The Model Prayer:

The Christian's Primer

Eli Landrum

Parson's Porch Books
www.parsonsporchbooks.com

The Model Prayer: The Christian's Primer
ISBN: Softcover 978-1-949888-94-2
Copyright © 2019 by Eli Landrum

All rights reserved. No part of this book may be reproduced or transmitted in any form or by any means, electronic or mechanical, including photocopying, recording, or by any information storage and retrieval system, without permission in writing from the publisher.

To the dedicated, insightful teachers who instilled in
me a love for the New Testament and an enduring
quest to understand and apply its truths

Contents

Introduction 7
The Correct Approach 13
Approaching God as Father 19
Expressing Reverence for God 30
Expanding God's Rule 42
Fulfilling God's Will 51
Asking for Bread 62
Requesting and Giving Forgiveness 74
A Sobering Elaboration 87
Pleading for Protection 90
Offering a Concluding Doxology 100
Conclusion: Thoughts on Prayer 103
Postscript 106
Selected Bibliography 110

Introduction

Another Book?

The writer of Ecclesiastes noted that "there is no end to the making of many books" (Ecclesiastes 12:12).[1] His observation certainly applies to books on prayer. Why, then, another book that explores the prayer-pattern Jesus gave His early followers? That is a good question. After all, countless books have been written on the subject. Furthermore, vast numbers of sermons have been delivered based on the texts, and myriads of Sunday School lessons have examined the prayer. It has been put to music, and many of us are moved by its beauty. To undertake to write another book that explores the brief accounts may seem presumptuous, even somewhat arrogant. I do not presume to be a New Testament scholar, and I do not claim insights no one else has received. In fact, most of my understanding of Jesus' words come from insights teachers, preachers, and writers have expressed. I have undertaken to write out of a personal interest in and fascination with Jesus' teaching that is preserved for us in the Gospels of Matthew and Luke.

---

[1] Unless otherwise noted, all scriptural quotations are from the *CSB Study Bible (Christian Standard Bible* by Holman Bible Publishers, Nashville, Tennessee, 2017).

I long have been convinced that the title "the Lord's Prayer" is a misnomer. Most of those who use the title may well mean the prayer the Lord gave His followers. Some may take it to mean a prayer Jesus prayed and shared with His disciples. Yet the petition for forgiveness is evidence to me that Jesus did not pray the prayer but intended it to be a pattern used by His followers. He had no sin for which He needed forgiveness; we are sinners and constantly need God's mercy. I believe the best title for Jesus' outline is "the Model Prayer." To me, it is a pattern or framework— a guide to authentic and productive prayer.

I am profoundly impressed with the brevity of the prayer Jesus outlined. The economy of words is striking. The Greek text of Matthew has 56 words. Luke's account has even fewer. It truly is a "bare bones" outline. Yet, so much ground is covered. My prayers sometimes tend to be somewhat long and to follow a long-ago set outline, which has caused me to wonder whether God has gotten tired of and bored with them. My faith is that He endures them patiently. Jesus' framework is succinct; it is to the point.

I am awed by the prayer's scope. It moves from praising God to the concerns of the person praying to a plea for mercy to a petition for protection from temptation and evil. Interpreters have noted that the Model Prayer has six petitions. The first three relate to

God, His kingdom, and His will. The next three relate to His people.

I have great admiration for Jesus' genius in crafting a prayer that is easily committed to memory. The framework can be brought to mind at any time and can be used as a guide to personal and public prayers. It can be a beautiful and significant part of genuine worship, personal and corporate. It can deepen an individual's personal relationship with God, and it can strengthen the bonds of fellowship in a community of faith.

Memorization can be a tremendous benefit, but it also presents a danger: We can repeat the words of the Model Prayer without giving any real thought to them—without considering the gravity and implications of nearly every word. We can recite it by rote. If we carefully weighed the words, how many of us could honestly repeat them? Saying the prayer is one thing; making it ours is quite another. Thoughtless repetition has no meaning or real effect. In the case of the prayer-pattern, familiarity breeds lack of concentration on the words' import. When we offer it in sincerity and deep commitment, it becomes a vital part of worship.

I think we have to keep in mind that in one sense, Jesus' model is comprehensive in that it includes proper reverence for God and participation in His redemptive purpose and addresses human need. In another sense, however, it is a framework that invites expansion. It is as though Jesus left it to us to flesh out His pattern. The model includes no intercession for others, no expressions of gratitude for blessings received, no thankfulness for grace, and no petitions for healing, which we often include in our prayers. What Jesus gave, I believe, was a starting point for prayer that progressively matures. We grow in praying by praying daily, listening to other believers' public prayers, and reading the prayers of devout Christians. So, to me, the Model Prayer is the beginning of a lifelong discipline. We are to move from the child's prayers "Now I lay me down to sleep...." and "God is great, God is good...." to more inclusive expressions of gratitude, intercession, and petition.

Setting the Scene(s)

The Model Prayer appears in Matthew 6:9-13 and Luke 11:2-4. Matthew placed it in a context dealing with prayer in the Sermon on the Mount. Jesus warned His disciples against praying as hypocrites did. Instead of standing in public places so passersby could see them praying and notice how religious they were, Jesus' followers were to go to a private place (what a good friend calls his "sacred space") and pray to the heavenly Father. Rather than receive people's accolades, they would receive God's reward. Jesus also warned against imitating Gentiles' lengthy prayers in which their wordiness was designed to ensure they would be heard and answered. God was aware of believers' needs, implying that He would supply those needs. Then Jesus gave the authentic alternative way to pray.

Luke placed a shorter version of the Model Prayer in an intriguing context. At an unspecified time and place during Jesus' ministry, He paused to pray. Whether or not He prayed aloud, and the disciples heard Him, they did not interrupt Him but waited for Him to conclude His prayer. Then they asked Him to teach them to pray as John the Baptist had taught his followers. Rabbis customarily provided their disciples with brief guides for prayer. No doubt Jesus' disciples were acquainted with prayers as a part of synagogue worship and likely recited those prayers with other worshipers. Yet evidently something about Jesus' praying was fresh and unique. Thus, they wanted to pray as He did. According to Luke, Jesus gave them a brief, condensed pattern for prayer.

Some interpreters suggest that Luke's version of the Model Prayer is the oldest or original form. In this view, under divine inspiration, Matthew expanded the prayer by adding interpretations. One example of this occurrence is in the two writers' accounts of one of Jesus' beatitudes. Luke wrote "blessed are you who are poor" (Luke 11:20), while Matthew wrote "blessed are the poor in spirit" (Matthew 5:3). No violence is done to Jesus' words; in fact, we are presented with divinely inspired clarity.

One view of the two somewhat differing prayer-frameworks is that Jesus gave them on two different occasions. In this approach, Luke's account reflects a time later than the account in Matthew.

The differing settings for the Model Prayer need not trouble us. Most likely, the writers exercised freedom in arranging their Gospels. They did not write chronological biographies but arranged their materials to achieve their individual purposes for writing. Whatever the setting, Jesus gave His followers a marvelous framework for prayer. Each of the Model Prayer's words and phrases deserves and demands careful attention and application. Together, we will seek to do so as we reverently and humbly examine Jesus' marvelous gift to us: a guide for authentic and effective prayer.

The Correct Approach

I was a much younger Christian then, but I still remember the first time I heard an older adult Christian, who had been a believer for decades, ask God in his public prayer to teach him and other believers how to pray. I was taken aback, and I thought he always did a good job leading in prayer. Surely, he knew how to pray. Through the years since that time, I have come to understand his petition. I repeatedly have asked my heavenly Father to teach me to pray. I have asked that I pray rightly, and I have asked forgiveness if I have not done so. He received me into His family of faith more than 70 years ago, and I still make those requests.

Prayer is an indispensable part of our lives as God's children through our faith-commitments to Christ. The Father does not need to hear from us nearly as much as we need to talk with Him daily. We dare not neglect prayer, for our lives are strong or weak in proportion to our regular conversations with God. Prayer is His gracious gift that allows us to be constantly in touch with Him, and it allows us to draw from His inexhaustible resources of love, mercy, and grace. Through prayer, the Christian speaks to God and allows God to communicate with him/her. Patiently awaiting His response is as vital as expressing wants and needs.

Jesus set the ultimate example of effective praying by His acts of talking with His Father at key points in His life and ministry. He prayed at His baptism by John the Baptist. Luke wrote: "When all the people were baptized, Jesus also was baptized. As He was praying, heaven was opened, and the Holy Spirit descended on him in a physical appearance like a dove" (Luke 3:21-22a). Before He chose the 12 men who would comprise the group who would follow Him most closely, He prayed. Luke wrote: "During those days he went out to the mountain to pray and spent all night in prayer to God. When daylight came, he summoned his disciples, and he chose twelve of them" (Luke 6:12-13a). He sometimes sought solitude to pray. Mark wrote that on one occasion "very early in the morning, while it was still dark, he got up, went out, and made His way to a deserted place; and there he was praying" (Mark 1:35). John wrote that before Jesus raised Lazarus from death, "Jesus raised his eyes and said, 'Father, I thank you that you heard me. I know that you always hear me, but because of the crowd standing here I said this, so that they may believe you sent me'" (John 11:42). Before His arrest, He spoke His magnificent High Priestly prayer in John 17, in which he interceded for His disciples and all future believers. In His remarkable prayer in Gethsemane, He prayed: "*Abba*, Father! All things are possible for you. Take this cup away from me. Nevertheless, not what I will, but what you will" (Mark 14:36). Then, from the cross He prayed, "Father, forgive them, because they do not know what they are doing: (Luke 23:34).

In His life and ministry, Jesus magnified the need for prayer to God, the way to pray, and the spiritual strength to be gained from consistent prayer. If God's unique Son considered prayer to be a vital part of relationship with God and a necessary source of power for living, how much more should we view the channel of prayer as imperative for us?

With the realization of our need to pray should come the understanding that prayer is not merely or solely a religious exercise. Neither the people praying, nor their prayers, bring the requested results. That is, beautifully phrased prayers and our degree of devotion do not leverage favorable response. God, to whom we pray, answers in His infinite wisdom and in His power applied in compassion. One glaring key is the attitude of the person praying.

The Model Prayer Jesus gave His disciples is perhaps the best-known and most loved of all recorded prayers. Many of us have committed it to memory. In fact, it is the only prayer some people employ. It is included in corporate worship and in private devotions. Yet, I sometimes wonder how many worshippers merely repeat the words without probing their meaning. How many realize the reason Jesus spoke the words? From what source did this magnificent model arise? What do the petitions mean to the person saying them by rote, and how often do the words lead to actions?

One rule of life is that repetition can empty of meaning the most beautiful and challenging words. This is especially true of well-known literary pieces. Rote memory can convert beautiful prose or poetry into mere recitation. On the verge of entering high school, my class was given the assignment of memorizing Lincoln's Gettysburg Address. Dutifully, I did so. For a while I could repeat it verbatim. Yet for a long time it remained a recitation. I since have come to appreciate the deep emotion behind the words, the determined will expressed, and the clarion call to faithful duty to preserve our nation's unity. Merely reciting the Model Pray, most often called "The Lord's Prayer," can empty it of its intended meaning.

I believe that no magic is evoked by repeating "The Lord's Prayer." One day, during an interlude in the process of writing, I was watching the news reports on one of our local television stations. As a teaser before a rather lengthy commercial break, the commentator said that coming up was a woman's account of being saved by the Lord's Prayer. I waited impatiently through seemingly endless commercials for her to talk about her experience. When the news resumed, the woman told about a random gunshot that sent a bullet though the wall of the room where she was. If the bullet had not ricocheted off a plaque on which the Lord's Prayer was inscribed, the bullet would have struck her. A wall mounting altered the trajectory of a bullet but reciting the Model Prayer in desperation is no guarantee of rescue. It was never designed to be an automatic bail-out. Our knowing and reciting the words in any situation, even a severe crisis, does not compel God to answer; they do not give anyone special claim on God merely because the person praying uses words Jesus gave His followers. His words must become our words; His attitude, devotion to God, and His pure motives must be ours.

We need to keep in mind that the Model Prayer was part of basic instruction to people who were learning to relate to God on a new basis, in a new relationship of grace. Jesus' pattern of prayer was one of many starting points for them. In like manner, it is a starting point for us in talking with God. A second dictionary definition of the word *primer* is "a textbook that gives the first principles of any subject." I think the first listed definition also applies to the Model Prayer: "a book for teaching children how to spell or read."[2] Applied to the study of the Model Prayer, the prayer is a primer for God's children.

---

[2] *Webster's New World Dictionary of the American Language*, p. 590.

We are helped to have a healthy view of the Model Prayer when we keep in mind that Jesus, our Lord and Savior, God's Son, gifted us with it. I have long been convinced that Jesus' words came out of His extended experience with His Father. To me, these were no spur-of-the-moment phrases. Out of His daily give-and-take with people, He was keenly aware of their needs: a constant, healthy respect for God; submission to His rule and will; a need for daily provision; a need to be forgiven and to forgive; and protection from evil.

A concentrated look at the Model Prayer causes us to marvel at its composition. Few works of prose and poetry are so beautiful in construction, flow, and phrasing. Everything is precise and to the point, and yet nothing essential to life with God is omitted. It is so interwoven and coordinated that it almost defies dissection in the process of study. The prayer gives attention to God, people, and things. In it, Jesus shows us how we are to be related to each of them.

In the Model Prayer are essential words of Jesus for His followers. They can lead to greater spiritual experiences and a closer relationship with the Father if we study them in the right spirit. We dare not merely discuss the prayer in an analytical, detached manner. It must become an integral inclusion in the fabric of our living.

Approaching God as Father

"Our Father" (Matthew 6:9)

Jesus introduced his model for Christian prayer with the words, "Therefore, you should pray like this" (Matthew 6:9). The term "therefore" reaches back to the markedly flawed prayers of hypocrites (mere play-actors) and Gentiles (non-Jews) against which Jesus warned in Matthew 6:5-8. What He would present was in stark contrast to those practices. The Greek word translated "should pray" actually is a command: "pray." The introductory words can be translated, "Therefore after this manner you yourselves (emphatic) are to pray."[3]

With the opening words of the Model Prayer itself, Jesus introduced His disciples—and introduces us—to a whole new realm of thought and rich experience. He taught that His followers can approach God as Father. The word "Father" had been applied to God before. This method of reference was not new. Yet, no one had ever taught people to approach God in this way. Jesus' emphasis was entirely original.

In the Old Testament, God is presented as Israel's Father. In Deuteronomy 14:1, Moses declared of the

---

[3] Archibald Thomas Robertson, "The Gospel According to Matthew" in *Word Pictures in the New Testament*, vol. 1, p. 52.

Israelites: "You are sons of the Lord your God." In Isaiah 63:16; 64:8, Israel is depicted as saying to God, "You are our Father." Through the prophet Hosea, God said, "When Israel was a child, I loved him, and out of Egypt I called my son."[4] By the exodus event, God had adopted the nation of Israel to be His son. A person who was fortunate enough to be born a Jew had God for his or her Father in the sense of being a member of the Jewish nation, the covenant community. In addition, the king in Israel was considered to be God's son in a special sense. The psalmist-king wrote concerning his coronation: "I will declare the Lord's decree. He said to me, 'You are my son; today I have become your Father'" (Psalm 2:7). In Jesus' time, rabbis addressed God as Father in their prayers.

The basic Jewish concept of God as Father likely served as the basis of Jesus' use of the term. His frequent use of the word "Father," however, was distinctive, unique. Jesus spoke of God as His Father and His followers' Father. No one before Him had used the term "Father" to refer to God so many times and with such deep meaning and warm intimacy.

The Greek word Jesus used for "Father" expresses the ideas of one who is nourisher, protector, and upholder.

---

[4] Hosea 11:1.

It was used to indicate the parental male and more distant ancestors. Jesus likely spoke in Aramaic, using the word *Abba,* which best may be rendered "Daddy" with overtones of warmth and intimacy. The word carried the sense of a child's love for and trust in his/her father.

Today, many children have the tremendous advantage of having fathers or father-figures who are (or were) loving, kind, patient, and protective. These fatherly individuals provide for their children's needs and are always "there for them." Sociologists have concluded that children of such fathers are likely to view God as being like their fathers. The children have healthy perceptions of God. To hear or read of Him as the heavenly Father stirs positive, warm emotions.

Jesus' use of the word "Father" in addressing God conveyed the sense of Fatherhood at its absolute highest and best—perfect or ideal Fatherhood. Tragically, not all children have had loving fathers and thus may have unhealthy perceptions of Him. Some have grown into adulthood never having heard their fathers express love for them. Some fathers were abusive, cool, aloof and detached, overly controlling, or absentee. For some people, to hear or read the word "father" causes disturbing memories and raw emotions to surge to the surface. To call God "Father" is to approach One who is loving, compassionate, kind, and deeply caring. We can trust Him to do what is best for us.

With His use of the word "Father," Jesus emphasized that relationship with God is deeply personal. God relates to His people one-to-one, and He does so with deepest care and concern. The term "Father" would be highly suggestive to Jesus' disciples. In the Jewish family, the father was the undisputed "head of the house" and had absolute authority. Yet the best Jewish fathers provided for all members of their families, caring intensely for each of them. Such fathers loved their children and received the children's honor, obedience, and love. These fathers applied their strength and authority in love for their families' best interests. In essence, Jesus said to His disciples, "You may call God your Father. He exercises absolute authority, but He does so in love. You may look to Him for provision in the assurance that He cares for you personally, individually." Today, as we address God as Father in our prayers, we must do so with the recognition that we have that privilege because Jesus said so. We must understand the profound gift that is ours due to God's sheer grace. In looking again at Jesus' marvelous prayer-model, I have asked God to forgive me for the numerous times I have begun my prayers with "Father" or "our Father" without thought of the reason I can do so and the words' profound implications.

Worth noting is the essential truth that with the term "Father," Jesus emphasized that God is infinitely more than an impersonal power, a force in the universe, a principal, or a "first cause." God is Person and personal. Out of sheer grace, the Creator and Sustainer of the universe and the Provider of our redemption chooses to relate to us in love. Thus, to call God "Father" carries the forces of confession of His sovereignty and gratitude for who He is.

With the phrase "our Father," Jesus taught His disciples that God is approachable. God is keenly interested in His children, even as the best earthly fathers are intensely interested in their children. "Father" is a warm and tender address for One who has time to hear His children's requests, for He holds them to be of highest importance, worthy of His undivided attention. To me, few scenes are as touching and meaningful as the sight of a busy father who pauses to stoop and give his focused attention to his child's question or account, no matter how small or trivial it might seem. The child's confidence in this person who is, in the child's eyes, towering and strong, grows because the father stops to listen, honoring his child's approach. Jesus stressed that God's children can approach Him without fear of reproach.

Two images of fathers' attention to their children have become imprinted on my memory. Years ago, as I was shopping in a mall, I noticed a young father holding his little daughter. They were face-to-face (more precisely, nose-to-nose). She held his face in her small hands and was looking into his eyes as she spoke to him. In turn, he was listening intently. Since I chanced to see that tender scene, it has remained a human example of God's attentiveness to His children.

The second image that remains vivid to me was a photograph of John F. Kennedy at his desk in the Oval Office. The photographer was in front of the desk, and underneath in the open space was John-John, the president's little son. While his father worked, the boy played, comfortable in the presence of the world's most powerful leader. To John-John, he was Daddy, not Mr. President into whose presence not everyone had access. Through His sheer grace, God's children have access to him.

We need to be clear on two truths that have to do with God as Father. The first is that God was (and is) the Father of Jesus in a unique sense not available to us. In what is one part of the mystery of the Incarnation, Jesus was always acutely aware of His sonship to God, often referring to God as "my Father." Jesus was uniquely God's Son, the only one of His kind. Thus, in a lesser but real sense, we are God's children through faith. Jesus is His Son; we are sons and daughters.

The second truth is that God is not the Father of all people in the sense that Jesus had in mind. The reference to God as "the Father of all mankind" must be limited to God as the Creator of life. Jesus instructed His followers to address God as "our Father." He was speaking to people who had placed their faith in Him—believers. The Father-child relationship He taught involves more than our being creatures. Even in the earthly father-child relationship, much more than physical descent is involved. On the father's side, love, care, provision, and right use of authority are necessary for quality fatherhood. On the child's side, love, obedience, and respect are integral facets of real relationship.

God is the Father of people who have become His children through faith-commitments to Christ. He becomes Father when asked to become so, when we ask to become part of His family. In the chorus of the hymn "A Child of the king," Harriet E. Buell joyfully exclaimed: "I'm a child of the King, /A child of the King: /With Jesus my Savior, /I'm a child of the King." [No. 555, *The Baptist Hymnal,* 1991] When we ask God to become our heavenly Father, a spiritual relationship is established in which God directs and we follow; God calls, and we answer; God commands and we obey. In this new relationship, all the Father's resources are available to us; the Father shares all He has with us. We cease to be mere creatures and become children of the compassionate, attentive Father. God becomes more than Creator to us; He is Father is the highest, truest sense.

I feel strongly that our addressing God as Father should always have the undercurrent of wonder, amazement that He would want us to become His children and would go to extreme lengths to make that possible. The Apostle John expressed such wonder in 1 John 3:1: "See what great love the Father has given us that we should be called God's children—and we are!" Only because of God's sacrificial, self-giving love demonstrated in Christ can we become members of God's family. That realization should deepen our awe as we approach God.

The Father-child relationship is one facet of the abundant life of which Jesus spoke in John 10:10. Creaturehood is changed into the stature of children when God is made Father through faith. As creatures, each of us has access to the physical resources of God's world. As His children, we enter into an intimate relationship in which we are made heirs to all that is His. He gives us His kind of life, which cannot be altered or taken away.

For people who enter God's family through faith, another realization surfaces. In Matthew 10:29-31, Jesus reminded His disciples that sparrows could be bought cheaply, yet God took notice of each one that fell to earth. He assured His followers they were worth many sparrows. What a striking, memorable way to emphasize that God knows and values each of His children! One line of a beautiful song proclaims joyfully, "His eye is on the sparrow, and I know He watches me." The psalmist was awed by the thought that God cares about people: "What is a human being that you remember him, a son of man that you look after him?" (Psalm 8:4).

Helmut Thielicke, a German scholar and preacher, preached a series of sermons on the Model Prayer during the dark days of World War II. He wrote: "Only in him (Jesus) can we ever know the secret that the Father's voice is really and truly calling our name in the dark forest and that we can answer as beloved children: 'Abba! Father!' "[5] In the wind, rain, thunder, and lightening of this life, we hear One pass by who knows us by name and calls to us. In the din, roar, and rush of our daily living, we hear One whom to know is life. Jesus assured His followers that as the Good Shepherd, He knows His sheep and calls them by name (John 10:3). God's child is never lost in the crowd. Our Father knows our names.

---

[5] Helmut Thielicke, *Our Heavenly Father: Sermons on the Lord's Prayer*, p. 29.

Significantly, Jesus began His prayer-outline with the phrase *"our* Father." (Italics mine.) Luke did not include the word "our" and began simply with "Father" (Luke 11:2). Nowhere in the prayer-pattern do the words "I," "me," and "my" appear. The terms "our" and "us" do occur. From the outset, Jesus stressed that His model is a fellowship prayer. Children who have the same Heavenly Father and make their requests of Him share life—and new life—on the deepest level. We miss a significant point of emphasis when we fail to realize that the opening words of the prayer-guide, as well as the repeated plurals, are a stimulus to fellowship and unity of purpose. When we join together in saying "our Father," we acknowledge meaningful relationship; we recognize one supreme authority; we share a never-failing love and acknowledge membership in one spiritual family. The words remind us, as often as we read or say them, that we all are children of the same Father. Any time we pray the Model Prayer, we should be reminded that as believers we are sharers in a community of faith, both local and world-wide. We are brothers and sisters in Christ.

Earlier in the Sermon on the Mount, Jesus had taught that if His listeners were to take their gifts to the altar and remember that individuals had something against them, the would-be worshipers were to first go and be reconciled with the offended people. Then the worshipers were to offer their gifts (Matthew 5:23-24).

In like manner, we well may need to repair relationships in the community of faith before we can pray the Model Prayer.

As I contemplated again the opening words of the Model Prayer, it occurred to me that in incredibly succinct fashion, Jesus emphasized what theologians have described as our vertical and horizontal relationships. He placed first our relationship with God and our relationship with other believers. My guess is that Jesus not only had spent a lot of time praying but also contemplating the importance of prayer's being inclusive.

The Model Prayer's first words teach us that God's children by grace through faith can approach Him and that He is present to hear and to respond. He knows us by name, cares for us, and is ready to listen intently to us. Moreover, we are to include our spiritual brothers and sisters in our prayers.

Expressing Reverence for God

("Our Father) in heaven, your name be honored as holy" (Matthew 6:9).

With the Model Prayer's opening words "Our Father," Jesus set the tone for our relationship with God. God will be Father to people willing to become His children through the exercise of their choice in total trust. They can approach Him, and He will give individual attention it each one, who in turn must see himself/herself as a member of a community of faith, a family.

In the words that follow the initial phrase, Jesus struck a perfect balance in His followers' addressing God and conversing with Him. Jesus addressed the Father "in heaven" and asked that His "name be honored as holy." In so doing, Jesus emphasized that believers who would approach God must do so with deepest reverence. Our being allowed to say "our Father" must not deteriorate into careless familiarity with God. God chooses to relate to us in an intimacy of deepest sharing, but we can never confuse intimacy with presumption; we cannot diminish our relationship with Him by presuming on Him. Conversation with the Infinite must be approached and conducted with respect and awe. The One who chooses to be the Heavenly Father is also holy. Finite humans may speak with their Creator with confidence. As the writer of Hebrews stated, as Christians we can "approach the throne of grace with boldness (confidence), so that we may receive mercy and find grace to help us in time of need" (Hebrews 4:16). As we will see, confidence is vastly different from brashness or flippancy. God demands and deserves respect. Jesus strongly emphasized that God is worthy of reverence.

The phrase "in heaven" is a guard against over familiarity with God. He is Father, but He is much more. Luke did not include the phrase in his account. Matthew's inclusion cautions against any brashness or casualness in approaching God. He is sovereign, the Ruler of the universe and particularly of believers. Whether heaven is "up there," "out there," or "here" as another dimension, God is separate from, other than, humans. He is "seated on a high and lofty throne," as the prophet Isaiah declared (Isaiah 6:1). That is, He is exalted, supreme Ruler. Whether or not He literally sits on a throne, He is to be approached with cautious awe. Theologians have a five-dollar word for what Isaiah stated: God is transcendent. The dictionary definition of the term is "surpassing," "excelling." God is above and beyond humans and the created universe.

In a context dealing with God's gracious pardon for repentant sinners, through the prophet Isaiah God emphasized His separateness or otherness, His uniqueness. God said: "My thoughts are not your thoughts, and your ways are not my ways. This is the Lord's declaration. For as heaven is higher than the earth, so my ways are higher than your ways, and my thoughts than your thoughts" (Isaiah 55:8-9).

The Scriptures make clear that the transcendent God also is imminent; He is present and active in human history and in His children's lives. He is no distant God who has removed Himself from His creation and His highest creatures.

The phrase "your name be honored as holy" requires close examination and careful implementation. In Hebrew thought, the word "name" meant much more than a title or label. It meant the individual's character, integrity, and personality. For example, the name Joshua, from which the name Jesus is derived, means "Yahweh (God) saves." Those names aptly characterized both men. The name Noah means "comfort." The name Malachi means "my messenger." Examples could be multiplied, but the major emphasis is that to the Jews the word name meant a person's basic self. Thus, God's name means His character, integrity, and active power—His self or Person.

The Scriptures reveal that God is all-powerful, all-knowing, and present everywhere. The writer of Psalm

103 stated his insight that God is also compassionate: "As a father has compassion on his children, so the Lord has compassion on those who fear (reverence) him" (Psalm 103:13). We can be eternally grateful that in Jesus God made known a great deal more about Himself. Jesus demonstrated that God is love and loving, gracious, merciful, patient, kind, and faithful. Yet I am convinced these character-traits we can know are only a small window on all of who God is. He retains a great deal of mystery concerning Himself.

A popular preacher of a former generation presented an insightful and helpful analogy concerning God's revealed and yet largely veiled greatness. He noted that we can stand on a beach and view the waves breaking on the shore and the sea stretching to the horizon. Beyond our range of sight, however, lies an ocean whose magnitude is beyond our mental grasp. We observe merely the near part of it. In like manner, we view God's self-revelation in the Scriptures, in Jesus, and in history and understand something of who He is. Beyond our mental grasp, however, is the immeasurable reality of God's greatness.

I long have been intrigued with God's answer to Moses' question in Exodus 3:13-14a. Moses asked: "If I go to the Israelites and say to them, 'The God of your fathers has sent me to you,' and they ask me, 'What is his name?' what should I tell them?" God replied to

Moses, "I AM WHO I AM." The term translated "I AM" is actually YHWH. With vowels added, it is Yahweh. Various meanings have been suggested: "I cause to be," "I am who I have been," "I will be who I have been," "I will be who I will be." In essence God said, "I will be who I choose to be, free to act as I will." I think the difficulty in translating the word and the various possibilities are as God intended. That is, no one name can capture God's magnificent, superlative character.

Most of us are familiar with a story that has circulated for a number of years. A little girl was busily drawing on a sheet of paper. An adult asked her what she was drawing. She replied she was drawing a picture of God. With a note of surprise, the person told the girl that no one knows what God looks like. Without pausing or looking up, she said: "They will when I finish."

I long have been puzzled and somewhat incredulous that artists and cartoonists have attempted to paint or draw likenesses of God. Most of the portrayals I have seen present Him as an older man. As I was writing this, I went on the internet and pulled up Michelangelo's painting "The Creation of Adam." On the left side of the painting is the depiction of Adam as a solidly built, handsome young man. On the right side, God is depicted as a sturdy, older man with grey hair and beard, reaching out a finger toward Adam. I have wondered whether such art, as magnificent as it is, has given rise to the mental picture of God as a grandfatherly figure who is a somewhat larger-than-life human male. Today, God sometimes is referred to as "the Man up there" or "the man." Even if He is addressed as Man or MAN, we do Him a disservice. He is not merely more than us—a larger version of a human male; He is totally other than us.

We know something about God because He has chosen to make Himself known partially—more than enough to reveal that His character is redemptive. He comes to us with the offer of relationship with Him that entails His forgiveness and our commitment to Him. We can trust, love, and serve the God revealed most completely in Jesus.

The Greek word rendered "be honored as holy" literally is "let be regarded or reverenced as holy." Jesus indicated His followers were to pray that God would receive the reverence, respect, or awe due Him. The term "holy" has the idea of separation, of acknowledging something or someone to be sacred and treating it or the person as such. William Barclay noted that the meaning of the Greek word for holy is "different." Applied to God, it has the sense of His belonging to "a different sphere of quality and of being."[6] Helmut Thielicke wrote that Jesus included the words in Matthew 6:9b in His model prayer so His followers might recognize fully the One with whom they converse when they pray. God and humans must be put into proper perspective. He who is Divine Designer of complex human life and of the little planet we inhabit must be approached in humility. We have no innate right to approach Him in prayer; in fact, to do so we first must ask for His cleansing. Flawed, weak, sinful humans can enter His presence and talk with Him only because of His grace extended to us.

In Psalm 8:5, the psalmist marveled that God had created human beings "a little less than God." This was not a boast but was an expression of absolute amazement. Thus, we cannot fall prey to the notion that we are almost on God's level. It can become all too easy to bring God down to our level, to almost view Him as one of us. We need to constantly remind ourselves that in the psalmist's words, God "made" us the highest of His creation. The writer of Genesis stressed that "God created man in his own image; he created him in the image of God; he created them male and female" (Genesis 1:27). Whatever the phrase "the image of God" means, to me it at least means that humans have self-consciousness, memory, the ability

---

[6] William Barclay, *The Beatitudes & The Lord's Prayer for Everyman,* p. 177.

to make intelligent choices, the capacity to plan and project concerning the future, and the ability to form relationships. I definitely do not believe we bear a physical resemblance to God. If we are not careful, we can forget we are made; we can begin to form God in our image. The danger is that to some people God can become a magnified human, a little stronger and wiser than we are. With this misconception, no reason exists to approach God with deep respect.

Make no mistake about it: What is involved is a matter of respect. We are not likely to call on a God for whom we have little or no respect—except in cases of emergency. When I started out in the pastoral ministry, I was concerned to include good illustrations in my sermons. Thus, I bought a number of books that contained vast numbers of illustrations. (Happily, I later discovered that the best illustrations come out of personal experience.) One illustration concerning prayer has remained lodged in my memory. A fisherman was in his small boat in the middle of a lake when a storm arose. Rain came down in sheets, and the wind began to blow violently. The fisherman became desperate and began to pray. In essence, he prayed: "Lord, you know I haven't bothered you for a long time with my prayers. I promise you that if you get me out of this mess, I won't bother you again for another long time." I think I can safely state that the Model Prayer was not designed to be a crisis-prayer but a guide for consistent prayer in which we approach God with careful awe.

Not only will we be unlikely to approach sincerely and expectantly a God for whom we have little or no respect, but we also are not likely to listen to and respond positively to Him. "Your name be honored as holy" means "May you receive the deepest respect of which people are capable." Malcolm O. Tolbert wrote: "Men can fail to honor [God] as God. They show their disrespect for him in many ways. They ignore him, rebel against him, are profane and evil."[7] Honoring God is one of the glaring needs of our time.

We say—and rightly so—that respect must be earned, not merely demanded. Respect must be deserved. A person must prove his/her ability, use authority rightly, and display solid character. As we often hear or say, an individual must present his/her credentials. What are God's credentials? Why does He deserve utmost respect? His creation of infinitely more than we have been able to discover and comprehend would be more than enough. In addition, humans, in their complexity and vast potential, display the handiwork of a Master Craftsman. The supreme reason, however, for our deep respect for God arises out of a recognition of His redemptive work for us. That the Creator would visit

---

[7] Malcolm O. Tolbert, *Good News from Matthew*, vol. 1, p. 56.

this planet in human form, giving Himself no advantage, is startling enough. That He would give Himself in love to redeem us staggers the mind. One too big for our minds to grasp, holy and majestic beyond description, invites us into relationship with Him that will stretch into eternity. Such love and grace should cause us to bow before Him in reverence.

In addition to offering God our continuing sincere reverence, praying "your name be honored as holy" is to assume our role of influencing people to regard God as worthy of respect. We live in a time when God's name—the word and the revealed character it signifies—is anything but hallowed. The Jews came to view the name YHWH as so highly sacred that in writing and speaking, they substituted other terms. Many in our day have swung the pendulum to the other extreme. We often hear God invoked in the strongest curse word possible. Even some "religious" people speak of Him as though He were a heavenly vending machine spewing out delectable goodies on demand—or as though He were their confidant speaking especially to them. The list of ways people disrespect God could reach great lengths. Anything we do or say that makes Him commonplace and less than He is demonstrates a lack of respect.

We can influence people to reverence God as we reverence Him. Our lifestyles, observed and unobserved, should demonstrate an awareness of God's holiness and sovereignty. What we do consistently and the manner in which we go about our daily living should show an awareness of His presence and a healthy respect for Him. Our way of living can offer solid evidence that God can change lives redemptively—that new life in Christ is distinctively different in a positive sense. We should be in the process of reflecting more of His character as we understand it, which means we will be progressively more loving, gracious, merciful, and compassionate.

Our actions can influence people to revere God. When we move to help people in need, extend forgiveness, and share our stories of how we came to place faith in Christ, we can move people to respect the God we serve, the God who prompts us to act.

Our genuine worship is an expression of our reverence for God. Our consistent participation in collective worship is a testimony to our progressively pagan society that only one God exists and that He is worthy of our praise, obedience, and service. Such worship is an expression of our gratitude to One who has come to us in Jesus of Nazareth and who continues to express His love for us.

I long have believed strongly that we truly revere God when we show respect for other people—individuals created in His image as we are. We first demonstrate respect for God when we show respect for the lives He has given us to the extent that we consistently strive to make the most of them—when we take care of ourselves and seek to grow and develop. We respect God when we respect the earth He has given us by being good stewards of our environment. We respect God when we respect His church and the Scriptures He has inspired and preserved for us. I am inclined to believe that where there is little or no respect in these areas, there is little or no respect for God. Reverence for God is infinitely more than polite, pious words spoken in a religious setting. It involves our total lives dedicated to serving Him.

In the Model Prayer, Jesus taught that God's people can approach God and engage in dialogue with Him. God will hear and respond. We must, however, retain a sense of reverence for the Heavenly Father. We must honor his name (Himself) as holy, which means we must make Him the center of our lives.

Expanding God's Rule

"Your Kingdom come" (Matthew 6:10).

All four Gospels preserve the account. After Jesus' arrest and mock trial before the Jewish Sanhedrin, the Roman governor Pilate questioned Him. Pilate asked whether Jesus was the king of the Jews. Jesus replied: "Are you asking this on your own, or have others told you about me?" (John 18:34). After Pilate's response, Jesus declared: "My kingdom is not of this world.... If my kingdom were of this world, my servants would fight, so that I wouldn't be handed over to the Jews. But as it is, my kingdom is not from here" (John 18:36). He was not and would not be an earthly King.

Jesus previously had refused to be made an earthly king. Following His miracle of feeding more than five thousand people, the crowd proclaimed Him to be a prophet whom they had long awaited. "When Jesus realized that they were about to come and take him by force to make him king, he withdrew again to the mountain by himself" (John 6:15). The Jews held two views of the coming Messiah. The prominent view was that He would be a king after the order of David, a military conqueror who would vanquish the Jews' enemies and restore Israel's prominence and prestige. A second view was the Messiah would be a priestly deliverer. Jesus refused these images. Instead, He would be the Suffering Servant Messiah described in Isaiah 52:13—53:12 who would give Himself vicariously for the redemption of sinners.

Jesus did announce that with His coming, God's kingdom was breaking into history. John the Baptist, His forerunner, burst on the scene of history as Israel's first prophet in about 400 years. Matthew capsuled John's message: "Repent, because the kingdom of heaven has come near" (Matthew 3:2). Later, after John had been imprisoned, Jesus began His public ministry with the same ringing announcement (Matthew 4:17).

In an earlier book *(The Beatitudes: A profile of the King's Subject),* I stated my understanding of John's and Jesus' history-changing proclamation. The Greek word translated "repent" means "to undergo a change in frame of mind and feeling…to make a change of principle and practice."[8] From a change of mind the term came to mean a change of life's direction—an about-face from moving away from God to moving toward Him. Matthew's phrase "the kingdom of heaven" is a synonym for the phrase "the kingdom of God" and reflects the Jews' reverence for the name Yahweh, Israel's covenant God. They considered the name so sacred that they substituted other words for it. Both John and Jesus announced that in Jesus, God's

---

[8] *The Analytical Greek Lexicon,* p. 266.

kingdom had broken into human history. The Greek term rendered "has come near" has the basic idea of approaching, of being at hand. The sense is that God's kingdom was pressing in, so near as to be entering human history.

What did Jesus mean by God's "kingdom"? When we hear or read the word, we likely think of a territory or realm—a country ruled by a king or queen. We think of place, of land and boundaries. At one time, the United Kingdom was made up of various territories in different parts of the world. An often-repeated statement was that the sun never set over the British Empire. The kingdom of which Jesus spoke has nothing remotely to do with territory or realm.

God's kingdom is His sovereign rule over people—His kingship exercised in each life and over all of life. His is a beneficent rule to which people submit themselves willingly. God does not use His power to coerce submission but offers relationship with Him out of love and sheer grace. Individuals must choose to place themselves under His sovereignty and to accept His governing of all areas of their lives.

We need to be clear that the church and the kingdom are not synonymous. The kingdom is God's rule. In a special sense, the church is the collective people of God and, as such, is under God's rule, acknowledging

Him as Lord. This is true because individuals have submitted to God's rule; they have freely chosen to answer to Him in all of life. They acknowledge that this is His world, and He still has the definitive word concerning His created order. He also has the definitive word in His subjects' lives.

A hymn exhorts God's people to "worship the King, all glorious above, / And gratefully sing His wonderful love." ["O Worship the King, No. 16, *The Baptist Hymnal*, 1991] The words of a second hymn by an anonymous writer celebrates God's rule, recognizing that He is both King and Father. The hymn's first stanza is a joyous invitation of His people: "Come, Thou Almighty King, / Help us Thy name to sing, / Help us to praise: Father, all-glorious, / O'er all victorious, / Come, and reign over us, / Ancient of days." ["Come Thou Almighty King," No. 247, *The Baptist Hymnal*, 1991]

Of course, in a sense God rules whether or not people place themselves under His sovereignty. He rules over the entirety of His creation. Yet He becomes gracious, beneficent Ruler (and heavenly Father) in a special sense over people who believe He is, has made Himself known in Jesus, and warmly receives individuals who make faith-commitments to Christ. The ringing affirmation of the Scriptures is that God is sovereign; the question remains whether people will acknowledge that truth and become His subjects, the Heavenly Father's dearly loved children.

A great deal of Jesus' teaching had to do with the kingdom of God. In numerous parables, He explained what the kingdom is like. One resounding—and in a real sense ominous—note He sounded was the infinite value of entering the kingdom and the urgency in doing so. It is life's most crucial, pivotal decision.

We need to be clear on a crucial point: As believers, we do not "build" God's kingdom. God expands His kingdom; His rule comes to us as a gracious offer of life with Him. Frank Stagg wrote: "Not once does [the New Testament] speak of man as *building* the kingdom. It is God's alone to give or to establish; it is man's to await, to receive, to enter, and to proclaim."[9]

Jesus' petition "your kingdom come" is an imperative: "let your kingdom come." The form of the word Jesus used conveys a tone of urgency. Does this mean the kingdom is future, something for which we must wait and that is dependent on us? What do these words mean in the 21st century? Can this petition in the Model Prayer, spoken so long ago, maintain its relevance for a vastly different culture? I am convinced these words are as fresh, urgent, and compelling as when Jesus first spoke them. We need to have a clear understanding of

---

[9] Frank Stagg, *New Testament Theology*, p. 153.

what Jesus meant, and we need to make the petition ours in a deeply personal way.

Although some interpreters suggest this petition refers to a future completion at the end of history, I concur with those who emphasize that God's kingdom is present; He is at work among us to draw people to Himself with the offer of redeeming grace. God rules now; His rule will be universally acknowledged when Christ returns and the curtain of history falls. On one occasion, Jesus replied to a group of Pharisees who asked when the kingdom would come: "The kingdom of God is not coming with something observable; no one will say, 'See here!' or 'There!' For you see, the kingdom of God is in your midst" (Luke 17:20-21). With Jesus' coming and redemptive work, God's kingdom had arrived. In Jesus, God was inviting all people to come under His loving, compassionate rule.

The consummation or fulfillment of the kingdom will come at Christ's return, marking the end of human history. At that time all humanity, joyously as Christ's people or grudgingly and eternally too late by people who had stubbornly refused saving grace, will acknowledge God's sovereignty and His work of redemption through Christ.

In the phrase "your kingdom come," Jesus taught that His followers are to pray that all people become subjects in God's kingdom—that every person come under His loving rule. Each individual enters God's kingdom as a little child—in total trust and dependence. Only people whose lives are governed by God can pray "your kingdom come." To use this phrase is to be willing to shoulder one's load in inviting people into the kingdom. We who know by experience God's gracious and compassionate rule will want every person to make Him sovereign over their lives.

The petition that God's kingdom come keeps people's needs constantly before the one praying. It also should move us to do what we can to persuade people to place themselves under God's sovereign rule. If so, the petition changes us and inspires us. We have often heard and read—and perhaps said—that prayer changes things. Authentic prayer changes the person praying, who then can change circumstances. When prayer issues in a new understanding of God's redemptive purpose and of the needs of people around him/her, the one praying begins to change situations ("things"). To pray "your kingdom come" reaffirms our submission to God as absolute Lord and our willingness to be instrumental in bringing people into a new relationship of love and grace that gives peace and hope. In addition, the petition leads the one praying to be acutely aware that he or she is the King's son or daughter and must therefore live life with a bearing worthy of such a relationship. When I reflect on the truth that I am "a child of the King," as the hymn states, I should be motivated to ensure my life reflects well on Him.

In what ways can we be instrumental in advancing God's kingdom? Our doing so may be as simple as inviting non-Christians to Bible study or worship. It may be telling our story of placing faith in Christ. It may be ministering to hurting people in Christ's spirit and seizing the opportunity to communicate His grace, love, and care. Out of a sense of sheer amazement that God would love me even though I am unlovable and would accept me although I am unacceptable, I should be motivated to gladly serve my loving Father.

A paradoxical truth is that when people give up the claim to rule their own lives and bow to God's sovereignty, they begin to reign with Christ. That is, they begin to share in His reign. "Wanting to be king, [a person] is slave. Willing to be slave, [the individual] becomes king, but king only as in Christ, God's anointed, [the person] is made to reign."[10]

"Your kingdom come," then, is a request that God completely rule an individual's life and that all people submit themselves to His sovereignty so they might experience victorious living in relationship with Him. A paraphrase of Jesus' petition might be "Let Your

---

[10] Stagg, *New Testament Theology*, p. 169.

divine governing be a reality in all people's lives." It also must be our petition, backed by our willingness to be God's instruments in working toward that goal.

Fulfilling God's Will

"Your will be done, on earth as it is in heaven" (Matthew 6:10b-11a).

Jesus' third petition in the Model Prayer expresses believers' submission to God's overriding purpose in His world: "Your will be done." Interpreters have pointed out that the first three petitions deal with matters related to God. The first asks that God's self-revealed character be genuinely respected. The second requests that all people place themselves under His sovereignty. The third asks that God's purpose come to fulfillment. The logical progression is apparent: When people place themselves under God beneficent rule, they become instrumental in in bringing others into relationship with Him and in implementing His will.

The third petition does not appear in Luke's account. In essence, it is a restatement of the petition that God's kingdom come—that it be expanded as people come under His rule and that it be fulfilled at the consummation of history.

Jesus used "heaven" as a model, as a point of comparison. His followers were to request that God's will "be done on earth as it is in heaven." Heaven is where God is. In that state or dimension of existence,

God's purpose is perfectly realized; in His presence are love, joy, peace, and perfect obedience. I have come to believe firmly that life in God's immediate presence is beyond our comprehension. I think the descriptions in Revelation are John's inspired attempts to portray the beauty and perfection of life with God in eternity. In His presence, His people will maintain deep reverence for Him, celebrate His sovereignty, and joyfully do His will.

Jesus' petition that God's will be done on earth conveys the sad reality that His will is not being done in His world. We only need to read or view daily news reports to be constantly reminded that ours is a fallen world in which God is a non-factor in many people's lives. Whatever your interpretation is of Genesis 3, humans' propensity for evil is undeniable and flourishes. In my favorite comic strip, one of characters is a little girl who constantly comes up with a new philosophy of life. It might be "Who cares?" or "Why be bothered?" Today, too many people seem to have adopted the philosophy "My will." Jesus said, "God's will."

As an aside, in my research I came across an insightful suggestion concerning the phrase "on earth." Jesus may have intended the words to apply to the first and second petitions as well as the third. Reverence for God, acknowledgment of His rule, and the fulfilment of His purpose are perfectly realized in heaven; His people not only are to respect Him, be His obedient subjects, and do His will here and now but also are to influence people outside the kingdom to do so.

In a real sense, the petition "your will be done" (reach fulfillment) is a dangerous request. I think believers must take extreme care in voicing this petition. They must make the words theirs in a deeply personal sense. Whether or not we realize it, what we really say in this petition is "Let your will be done, first of all, in me." This means we are open to receive and to act on the indications God gives about the quality, direction, and actions of our living. It means that our personal preferences, opinions, and drives become secondary, subject to correction or complete abandonment because of what we understand to be God's will.

A great deal has been written about God's will in an effort to help people know and implement His will for them as individuals and for believers generally. One of the most popular and often-cited resources is Leslie Weatherhead's little book *The Will of God*. He suggested three facets of God's will: His intentional will, His circumstantial will, and His ultimate will. I do not presume to improve on Weatherhead's approach. My approach comes out of my experience of often struggling to understand and to carry out God's will for me.

To me, the broad strokes of God's will for all people are clear—what I consider to be His general will. His overarching will is that all people accept His provision of redemption in Christ's atoning death and experience His resurrection life, which is life to the full. As 2 Peter 3:9 states, God does not want (will) "any to perish but all to come to repentance." His will is that His children grow toward spiritual maturity and in the process increasingly reflect His revealed character. His will also includes their serving Him by serving others. In addition, a facet of His will is that His family be marked by love and unity of spirit and purpose. Jesus' answer to a question concerning the greatest Commandment is a good summary of God's will for all people: "Love the Lord your God with all your heart, with all your soul, and with all your mind.... Love your neighbor as yourself" (Matthew 22:37-38). To me, these words make forever impossible our saying that if we only knew God's will for us, we would do it. I have the distinct impression that we sometimes do not get particulars about God's will because we do not work at implementing the broad facets of His will.

In the Model Prayer, Jesus stressed that God has a purpose and direction for life. In their freedom to choose, people may opt to ignore or reject that will or purpose. The particular details of His will, especially for each person, may not always be clear. The broad outline, however, is. The question for believers is whether we will take seriously what we understand of God's purpose for us. What we must be quite clear about is that once we pray "your will be done," we commit to whatever way God leads us. We commit to the ongoing process of gathering the most and best information possible about the issues of our living and then acting on the clearest thinking we can do.

Jesus provided the best possible model for living out the petition in the prayer-pattern He gave His disciples. On a level impossible for us to attain but that remains the tension in which believers live, He was conscious of and committed to doing His Father's will for Him. In John 4:34, He told His disciples: "My food is to do the will of him who sent me and to finish his work." In John 5:30, Jesus said: "I can do nothing on my own. I judge only as I hear, and my judgment is just, because I do not seek my own will, but the will of him who sent me." In John 6:38, He stated: "I have come down from heaven, not to do my own will, but the will of him who sent me."

Of course, the most poignant example of the agony sometimes involved in doing God's will is Jesus' experience in the Garden of Gethsemane. There, He set the tone for every Christian in every age. In moments of crises and decision about self-giving at cost, the Christian's prayer becomes "not what I will, but what you will" (Mark 14:36). In this statement of submission, in life and in the prospect of death, the believer places his/her destiny in the hands of One who is capable, trustworthy, and faithful. This agonized submission of Jesus should forever prevent a flippant, thoughtless, careless recitation-by-rote of the Model Prayer's petition, "your will be done."

When I pray authentically that God's will be done, I express a willingness to take my place in the mainstream of His redemptive purpose. I make the words mine with the acknowledgment that the Father's will is always for the absolute best for His children. He wills what is good and beneficial. I do not believe He wills what is threatening, harmful, and painful. To ascribe tragedy, injury, death, and disaster to God's will is, to me, to blame Him for acts He never commits. His will is for every believer's fulfillment in relationship with Him.

For example, God's will clearly is that people in the community of faith live in harmony and peace—to be bound together in unity of spirit and purpose. I clearly understand that God's design is complex. I am only a single thread in the pattern, but I take my place in order to add to the strength and beauty of the overall design.

How can we know God's will for us at various junctures in our lives? Years ago, a pastor-friend helped me establish a starting point in arriving at God's will for me. My pastoral internship was winding down. Two churches had expressed interest in calling me as their pastor. My pastor had not-so-subtly indicated I should accept one of the opportunities so he could hire a new staff member. I was not sure which was God's will for me, or whether either was the right one. One day over lunch I asked a friend who was pastor of another church in the city how he determined God's will for him. The gist of his response was that God had never directed him with an audible voice. He said he gathered as much information as he could about the specific situation, prayed for guidance, and made the decision he thought was right for him. He made an informed decision in which he trusted his intuition. I did as he did and decided to accept the call of one of the interested churches. As the course of my ministry unfolded, my choice was the right one.

Since that experience, I have been helped to add to the process of discerning God's will. I have become convinced His will is not a mysterious puzzle I must solve. Granted, determining His will in specific circumstances can be difficult. Two suggestions have helped me. When I cannot get a clear indication God's will, I seek to identify the need and opportunity nearest me and to act to meet it. Often, out of that response come further indications of His will. The second bit of counsel that has helped me is when I am not sure what God wills for me in light of a number of options, I can prayerfully settle on one and pursue it. If my choice turns out to be wrong, I can simply take another path.

I am convinced we can be certain of one truth when we think about submission to God's purpose: His will is that we live together in such a way that each person's highest good is kept in view. That means I begin to work for peace in the smallest circle of my relationships and move outward—from family to church to community. If I am not willing to work for peace in these areas, I cannot ask that God's will be done anywhere else by anybody else.

The phrase "your will be done on earth as in heaven" lays on every person who repeats it the responsibility of waiting to receive indications of God's will, putting himself/herself in motion to effect it, and attempting to lead others to a disposition that will allow God's will to be known and done in and through them. Many times, and perhaps most times, God's will does not come in a sudden flash of inspiration; it comes as a person struggles to be open to God's working. Sometimes, in the face of continuing silence, we must do the best we know to do.

The phrase "God's will" is often used, and it is often misused. Sometimes, people allow their wishes and God's will to become confused. Some use "the will of God" to cover actual motives that stem from their own self-centeredness. It can be used as a way out of tight places. Years ago, a fairly prominent pastor in my state had been a fellow student in seminary. More than once, I was told, he resorted to the use of God's will effectively. In his courtships, if he thought it best to get out while he could, he would tell the girl he felt it was God's will that they break off. The woman who became his wife must have beat him at his own game by saying emphatically she felt God's will was that they marry. He was not the only person to use God's will to serve his own purposes. Some well-meaning would-be comforters of people grief-stricken over the deaths of loved ones attribute the deaths to God's will. Not having ready explanations for the tragedies, these erroneous individuals resort to "God did it," adding to the emotional turmoil of the grievers. Sadly—and theologically incorrect, I believe—the phrase "act of God" is used to explain all manner of catastrophes. I strongly resist the notion that He wills and causes tragedy.

How are we to say the words "your will be done" in prayer? How do we say them many times? We can give several inflections to the petition. William Barclay suggested three attitudes we can adopt in repeating the words.[11]

---

[11] William Barclay, The Gospel of Matthew," vol.1, in *The Daily Study Bible*, pp. 213-214.

We may repeat the words in an attitude of resignation to the inevitable, a surrender to our fate. A. M. Hunter wrote: "We have turned the words 'Thy will be done' into a tombstone *cliché,* when Jesus meant them as a summons to God's servants to be up and doing— 'Thy will be done—and done by me!' "[12] Jesus' words are not meant to reflect a "whatever will be, will be" attitude. This petition is not to be wrung from a person by a feeling of helplessness, when one feels he/she has no other choice. It is to arise from the recognition that the One to whom he/she prays can lead in paths of righteousness and through valleys of deep darkness. This petition places life in His capable hands.

The third petition in the Model Prayer can be spoken in deep resentment, with the speaker resisting and rebelling, feeling overpowered, subdued, or cornered—with sagging shoulders and a muttered "alright, you win," as it were. The person may feel he/she is merely a puppet on a string, subject to the whims of an arbitrary power that cannot be resisted.

A person can repeat the words with love for and trust in the Father who cares for His children. Faith that rests in God's love, mercy, and grace is ready to receive and implement God's will.

---

[12] A. M. Hunter, *Teaching and Preaching the New Testament,* p. 94.

Repeating the petition that God's will be done on earth as it is done in heaven will not mean anything unless we make ourselves available to do what we understand of His will. In a real sense, it is a dangerous request, for He may make clear what He wants us to do, and it may not fit neatly into our projected plans.

Asking for Bread

"Give us today our daily bread" (Matthew 6:11b).

Several years ago, the teacher of our senior adult Sunday School class invited his neighbor to speak to us. The neighbor presented an informative lecture on the complex and mysterious nature of the human brain. He made no claims to understand fully this marvelous creation. His presentation was interesting and informative, but much of what he said went way over my head. I was captivated, however, by what he said about the little sensors in our brains that send signals to our digestive juices. The sights and smells of food activate the sensors so that we get ready to eat.

Few things make my mouth water more quickly than does the aroma of freshly baked bread. Loaves of sourdough bread or rolls fresh from the oven exert an almost magical, magnetic pull. Although I now have to be careful to count the carbohydrates I ingest, I enjoy fresh bread immensely. I readily understand the reason Jesus included the need for bread in the Model Prayer.

Two of the Model Prayer's intriguing characteristics are its brevity and the ground it covers. It can be offered in about a minute or less, but its scope is broad and inclusive. It begins with three petitions concerning God and His redemptive purpose. Then it moves to the concerns of the person praying. In effect, it moves from the greater to the lesser. Jesus indicated that the lesser—human need—is nonetheless important to God. Jesus' magnificent prayer-pattern demonstrates plainly that God cares about all of human life. He is concerned about people's sound spiritual life as well as their physical needs. All of life is significant and important to Him.

The order of Jesus' Model Prayer is noteworthy. First, God is to be given priority; He is to receive praise. When that is done, the person praying can turn to his/her needs. When the individual acknowledges God as Father, gives Him proper reverence, aligns himself/herself with God's redemptive purpose, and makes His will life's priority, that person can legitimately turn to personal needs. In fact, one suggestion about the petition's position in the Model Prayer is that only people who are committed to God's purpose and seek to fulfill it can legitimately ask for the means to do it.

Jesus stated that to ask God for what we need is valid; for us to ask for bread is OK. I wonder what our perception of God would be if Jesus had not included this petition. How would we be assured of our Father's concern for one of the largest areas of our living? Helmut Thielicke wrote that if God were not concerned with life's practicalities and needs—"little things"—we would be "fatherless" and "orphans." "Only a very small sector of our life would be considered worthy for God to dwell in." He insightfully noted that the greatest part of our lives would be relegated to "cold loneliness ."[13] Because Jesus included His followers' daily requirements in His Model Prayer, we can be confident of God's interest in our needs. He takes note of our struggles to get the basic elements necessary for our existence. This brief request is evidence that no part of our lives is unimportant to God. Bread plays a significant role in our lives. It is of vital concern to us, but is it not a small item to God? Because it is a genuine need in our lives, it has meaning to God. God is interested in the material, physical aspects of our lives. A person is not a body with a soul; the individual is a living soul, and God cares for the totality of each life.

To believe that God is deeply interested in all aspects of people's everyday lives is not to diminish Him. A man whose opinions I respected once told me his God was too big to be concerned with minute areas of people's lives. My reply then, and my firm conviction now, is that God is big beyond comprehension because He is so concerned; to me, His care for His creatures only adds to His greatness. He would be

---

[13] Thielicke, p. 80.

disappointingly small and inadequate indeed if our need of daily bread was of no concern to Him.

Jesus was well aware of the conditions of the time in His land. Many of His people scrabbled to eke out a living. Many if not most men were day laborers, seeking daily work wherever they could find it. They received a denarius for a day's work and were paid at the end of each day. If a laborer missed a day's work, his family faced the prospect of hunger until he could find work. Jesus' including the petition for daily bread was not a casual mention of something on life's periphery; it went to the core of human concerns. In our time, for many who live on the edge, it still does.

The word Jesus used for "bread" means "a loaf or thin cake of bread."[14] Flour was mixed with water and baked. The bakers made the bread in the form of an oblong or round cake of varying thickness. It could be as large as a plate or a platter.[15] The term could take on the wider meaning of "food of any kind."[16] Jesus may have had in mind a petition for a daily, adequate supply of food. A further suggestion is that the word encompassed all necessities of daily living.

---

[14] *The Analytical Greek Lexicon*, p. 53.
[15] Joseph Henry Thayer, *Greek-English Lexicon of the New Testament*, p. 75.
[16] Thayer, p. 76.

The fourth petition in the Model Prayer is difficult to translate properly. Interpreters vary on the proper rendering of the Greek word translated "daily." Suggestions include "necessary," "sufficient," "daily," and "for tomorrow." For many years, no other occurrence of the word occurred outside the Gospels of Matthew and Luke. Then, in more recent years, a fragment of a shopping list was discovered, and the word appeared on it. Based on this use, interpreters have argued that the term's meaning is "for the coming day." Thus, the petition in the Model Prayer would be "give us today our food for tomorrow." Perhaps all the various shades of meaning are present: "Give us the sufficient, necessary food for each day." The form of the word in Luke 11:3 could be translated "keep on giving us [bread] day by day."[17]

I have wondered whether Jesus intended the Model Prayer's fourth petition to remind the disciples of a familiar episode in the Jews' history. God had rescued the Israelites from bondage in Egypt, and as they journeyed through the wilderness the people became hungry and complained that Moses and Aaron had led them to a place where they would die from hunger. God told Moses He would "rain bread from heaven" for the people (Exodus 16:4). Each day, the people

---

[17] Frank Stagg, "Matthew" in *The Broadman Bible Commentary*, vol. 8, p. 115.

were to gather enough for that day. On the sixth day, they were to gather twice as much so they would not labor on the seventh day. I think Jesus well may have intended a comparison and a contrast. The comparison was that God was willing and able to meet His people's needs. The contrast was that the Israelites grumbled about lack of bread; Jesus' followers were to ask their heavenly Father for His supply. Petition, not complaint, was the proper attitude and approach.

Somewhere in my pastoral journey I ran across a brief story that I included in a sermon and that has stayed imbedded in my memory. During World War II, some people in a war zone in Europe were providing care for homeless children. The adults were giving the children shelter, food, clothing, and affection. Every night, however, most of the children would cry themselves to sleep. Nothing the caregivers did or said would stop the crying. Finally, one of the adults suggested that the children be given a piece of bread to hold when they went to bed. That solved the problem. What each child wanted was security—some assurance about the next day's food. Many people in our time are like children needing assurance of a piece of bread, there for them.

Jesus's suggested petition is a plea for necessary nutrition for each day. Two crucial truths stand out for me immediately. The first is that Jesus said "bread," not "cake and ice cream." For years, since the emergence of the pseudo "name-it-and-claim-it" theology, what I consider a severely warped concept of and approach to God and relationship with Him, I have had a running battle with people who promise prosperity for the faithful. Of course, prosperity is defined in terms of top jobs, massive income, lavish homes, and luxury cars. It usually hinges on "sowing a seed" (money, the more the better) into the hucksters' ministries, thus making those individuals wealthy.

What is glaringly lacking in the purveyors' messages is any idea of suffering, hardship, and sacrificial service in following Christ. Dedicated discipleship rarely if ever is mentioned. If relationship with God is a guarantee of accumulated wealth, Jesus missed it badly. When He died, His possessions were the items He wore. At no time did He amass material goods for Himself or promise His followers lives of luxury. Rather, He warned them of the high cost of following Him. His words to His disciples in Mark 10:29-30 have been severely twisted to support the prosperity (pseudo) gospel. His promise of "a hundred times more" than what they had given up to follow Him was overstatement to make the point that serving Him brought reward that cannot be measured, now and in the future. In our progressively decaying culture, faithfully following Christ is no "piece of cake." Most often, it is stubbornly going against the current.

The second truth that presents itself to me in the petition for bread is that life is to be lived one day at a time. I am aware that this is a rather trite truism often repeated. My guess is that your response goes along these lines: "That's trite. You can't live life any other way but one day at a time." Perhaps, but if you are like me, living one day at a time is difficult. Anticipations and concerns about tomorrow have a way of intruding on my todays. My day can be impacted by worry concerning the future. Later in Matthew 6, Jesus would instruct His disciples: "Don't worry (be overanxious) about tomorrow, because tomorrow will worry about itself. Each day has enough trouble of its own" (Matthew 6:34). In other words, "Concentrate on living each day to the full." The axiom "live one day at a time" contains a truth I cannot get away from. The petition for bread is a request for day-by-day provision, not for a lifetime security. No matter how we interpret the word "daily," the emphasis is on living today in trust in and dependence on God. The request solidly places each day in God's care—today and all the tomorrows.

That we have a clear grasp of the petition for daily bread is imperative. It is not a request for a heavenly handout; it is not to be voiced while we wait idly for provision to magically materialize—to "drop into our laps," as we sometimes say. In God's provision for the Israelites in the wilderness, the people had to expend the effort to gather the manna. Work was required on their part. William Barclay wrote: "[The plea in the Model Prayer] reminds us that prayer and work go hand in hand, that when we pray we must go to work to make our prayers come true."[18] We cannot be "freeloaders," attempting to mooch on God or other people. The petition for bread is not permission for us to be leeches or parasites. The petition is prayer-on-the-go, asking God's help while we make efforts to be part of the answer, while we take initiative and expend energy to earn bread. Indeed, the answer to our petition may come in the form of jobs, menial or otherwise.

During my long and seemingly unending journey as a seminary student, I received few provisions of "manna from heaven." Unlike one fellow student I knew, I had no benefactor who helped pay my way. What I did receive were two stints as interim pastor of a small country church and jobs that gained money enough for my needs. Prayer and initiative go together. Prayer and effort are productive.

The Model Prayer's fourth petition reminds us that all bread is God-given; we are dependent on Him for life and for all that sustains life. Without God's willingness to give coupled with our labor, no bread would be

---

[18] William Barclay, "The Gospel of Matthew," p. 219.

available. Both elements are essential. With people of insight, bread is an example of necessary cooperation between God and humans. Every loaf of bread can drive home the awareness that God's gracious disposition to give makes available the necessary ingredients; people's use of their energies and abilities allows them to combine the ingredients to produce the loaf. The same is true for our wider nutritional needs. We are utterly dependent on God, who works in and through us when we cooperate with Him. In our cooperative efforts, grasping and grabbing in greed have no place. Food for one day from the Father's hand is sufficient.

The request for bread serves as a preventative against deadly, insidious self-centeredness. Numerous commentators have pointed to and emphasized the pronoun: "*our* daily bread" or "*our* bread for tomorrow." The request for supplied need is a petition of fellowship and sharing. It becomes a prayer of human community, a prayer that all people receive sufficient food—and all other basic requirements of their living. To me, one implication is that the Christian community is to be active in meeting the needs of members living on the edge, without the basics. A second implication is that we do what we can to help others outside the company of faith.

I firmly believe we cannot pray for "bread" for ourselves with no thought of people with none and without being involved to some extent in relieving desperate need. Often, as my wife and I consider what we will eat at our next meal, a disquieting thought comes to me: While I am in the process of choosing *what* I will eat, many others are anxious about *whether* they will eat. My wife and I contribute to two organizations in our city that provide food for needy individuals and families, but what we give is a drop in the proverbial bucket. I live in the tension of needing to do more. The request for bread reminds us that we all are bound up together in the bundle of life, and selfishness has no place. Giving "bread" in the spirit of Christ has a definite place.

One of my favorite paintings hung on the wall of my study for years. It depicts a man at a table. Before him is a bowl of what may be soup or stew and a slice of bread. His head is bowed, and his hands are clasped before him. He is giving God thanks for his simple meal. The painting remains a constant reminder that I need to express gratitude for all that comes from my Father's hands as His provision. I must do more than "say a blessing." I must give sincere thanks.

Even as we include the petition for bread in our prayers, we must maintain an awareness that life consists of a great deal more than physical, material needs. We must, as it were, reach for the Father's hand as well as for the bread in it. In Matthew's account of Jesus' temptations in the wilderness, the first temptation was to use His power to turn stones to bread to relieve His hunger. Jesus responded: "It is written: Man must not live on bread alone but on every word that comes from the mouth of God" (Matthew 4:4). People are to live by the principles, directives, and guidelines God has revealed in the Scriptures. They are to live in a maturing relationship with the One who gives bread, a relationship marked by their faithfulness and obedience. He who gives must always remain elevated above the gift.

In a seemingly simple petition in the Model Prayer, Jesus opened up a wide range of thought. He said that without hesitation, we can ask our Father for our basic physical needs—and by implication warned that we are not to confuse needs with wants. Bread for one day, not desert, is what we can ask. Bread, representing life's material needs, is an important area of our living. It is important to us, and it is important to God. When He is given proper priority, and when we work in partnership with Him, we can approach the Father who cares for us with our requests. This gracious Provider is worthy of our trust, worship, service, and profound gratitude.

Requesting and Giving Forgiveness

"And forgive us our debts, as we also have forgiven our debtors" (Matthew 6:12).

My wife will back me up on this: I intensely despise debt. Throughout a long span of our married life, we had to do what myriads of couples have done: We incurred debt to make necessary purchases. When we married, I was slowly (and painfully) paying off a bank loan for my car. Later, as we purchased other cars, we borrowed money. When we bought our first house, we took out a loan. In all these instances, I fretted under the pressure of owing money. Getting out from under could not come fast enough, and when it happened it brought sweet relief.

In one situation of debt we experienced a sudden but more-than-welcome surprise. We had traded for a new car, but we did not have money to cover the full cost. My wife's parents readily loaned us the cash we needed without interest, and we began to make monthly payments to them. Shortly, "out of the blue," they told us they were canceling the debt. Growing up, I had heard the phrase "forgiving a debt," but until that moment I had not experienced such forgiveness. My in-laws' gracious act remains an acted parable of forgiveness on a spiritual level.

For me, the Model Prayer's fifth petition is the most difficult and demanding. It is not so difficult to understand; it is extremely difficult to do. I have no trouble with the first part of the request, for I am always aware of my need to be forgiven, and I repeatedly ask God to forgive me in the confidence He will do so. The second part is deeply unsettling because forgiving others does not come easily for me. Nevertheless, I live under the mandate of the One who has forgiven me and continues to pardon me and provide me with fresh starts.

The conjunction "and" is significant. It links the fifth petition with the preceding one. Being given daily provisions and both receiving and extending forgiveness are closely tied. Physical, material provision is necessary for our lives, and so are the experiences of being forgiven and forgiving others. In my view, the importance of the fifth petition and the difficulty involved in it are emphasized by the fact that in Matthew's account, it is the only request in the Model Prayer on which Jesus elaborated.

I honestly admit that I have times when I have to stay away from the Model Prayer's fifth petition. I do not believe I am not alone in this experience. At Robert Louis Stevenson's residence in Tahiti, his custom was to have daily family worship and to include in such worship the Model Prayer. On one occasion, as family members bowed to repeat the prayer, Stevenson got up and left the room. His wife followed him and asked if he were ill. "Is anything wrong?" "Only this" he replied, "I am not fit to pray the Lord's prayer today."[19] Sometimes, I know how he felt.

I once reviewed rather hastily the skirmishes I had experienced with people, the slights I had endured, and the minor hurts that had been inflicted on me. I issued a blanket forgiveness and felt good praying "forgive....as we also have forgiven." Since that early point in my life, through "the school of hard knocks," I have learned that when people inflict serious injury on me, I cannot quickly and easily say with sincerity, "I forgive." Yet Jesus' words will not let me escape the tension of being forgiven and with a recognition of that experience extending forgiveness to others.

The word Jesus used for "forgive" means "to send away," "to let go, or to give up, a debt."[20] It further means "to remit," "to pardon."[21] The Greek term for "debts" means "that which is justly or legally due," "offences"[22] and has the ideas of faults or sins.[23] It has the sense of moral obligation. The word "trespasses" that most often is used in repeating the Model Prayer

---

[19] Barclay, "The Gospel of Matthew," p. 224.
[20] Thayer, pp. 88-89.
[21] *The Analytical Greek Lexicon*, p. 62.
[22] Thayer, p. 469.
[23] *The Analytical Greek Lexicon*, p. 296.

"is a mistranslation made common by the Church of England Prayer Book."[24]

On a Sunday morning worship period in one of my pastorates, the congregation repeated the Model Prayer. I used the words "debts" and indebtedness, while everybody else used "trespasses" and "trespass." Afterward, the church organist made a point to chide me, not-so-subtly implying that I needed to memorize the prayer correctly. Turns out I was right. Nowhere in either account of the prayer does the Greek term for "trespass" occur.

In Luke's account of the Model Prayer, the petition reads, "And forgive us our sins, for we ourselves also forgive everyone in debt to us" (Luke 11:4). The word for "sins" means "to miss the mark." It is a shooter's word for failing to hit a target. The individual who sins against another misses God's high moral and ethical standard. Clearly, the debtor is a person who owes another, a delinquent debtor who has sinned against another. In this fifth petition, Jesus stressed our need to be forgiven and to be forgiving. We commit sin against God and others, and other people sin against.us.

---

[24] Archibald Thomas Robertson, "The Gospel According to Matthew" in *Word Pictures in the New Testament,* vol. 1, p. 54.

When we repeat the Model Prayer's fifth petition with sincerity and understanding, we confess that we are sinners, delinquent debtors to God. Periodically in our daily living, and most likely many times, we commit wrong. We wrong God, and we wrong others in any number of ways—by demeaning words, cruel actions, manipulation, inactivity in face of needs, and silence in the face of innuendo and false accusations. Perhaps worst of all, we too often are indifferent toward others. In all our indebtedness to God and our offenses against others, our sin always is primarily against God. Ultimately, all sin is against God. David, Israel's greatest king and a man after God's own heart, had committed adultery and was responsible for an innocent man's death. Confronted with his sins, in time David wrote a prayer, asking God for forgiveness. In his prayer, he confessed: "Against you—you alone—I have sinned and done this evil in your sight" (Psalm 51:4). He had sinned against others, but first and foremost, he had sinned against God. Basically, we are debtors to God. To say, "forgive us our debts," is a confession of being and doing wrong and a plea to be made right. In addition, as it is a communal prayer, it is an admission that the church is a community of forgiven sinners who go on needing periodic pardoning for sins.

Which one of us can say at this moment that all is right in our relationships with God and with other people?

Who can say he/she does not need to be forgiven and to forgive? We need to understand that forgiveness is not negative but is positive. It is not merely dismissing or sending away sin, wiping the slate clean. It definitely is that, but it also is bridging a chasm between us and God—a divide created by our wrong. The experience of forgiveness restores a relationship and sets the person on the right course. God grants repentant sinners a new start. In a real sense, the Christian life is marked by an endless stream of new starts. By our decisions, attitudes, and deliberate actions, we can remove ourselves from an intimate, effective relationship with God. We do not lose salvation, but we create distance between our Father and us. We move away from Him, deliberately or by casual drifting. Out of love and sheer grace, God can and will restore the relationship and enable us to resume the process of spiritual growth we have disrupted. This confidence, based on God's unchangeable character and faithfulness, gives us renewed incentive to please Him and to represent Him well as children who resemble Him in character. God is our Father who forgives when we meet His conditions of confession and repentance. We can be sure He does not take sin lightly. Because of the serious nature of wrong, forgiveness is always costly. Yet I am convinced God does not keep a heavenly ledger of black marks against us. When we acknowledge our indebtedness to Him and ask to be released from it, He discards our I.O.U.'s.

The older I grow, the more I hold on to Scripture passages that give assurance of God's readiness to forgive completely. The psalmist wrote: "As far as the east is from the west, so far has he [God] removed our transgressions from us" (Psalm 103:12). The prophet Jeremiah proclaimed that God would make a new covenant with His people and would "forgive their iniquity and never again remember their sin" (Jeremiah 31:34). The prophet Micah stated confidently, "He [God] will again have compassion on us; he will vanquish our iniquities. You will cast all our sins into the depths of the sea" (Micah 7:19). John, the aged apostle, wrote to early Christians: "If we confess our sins, he is faithful and righteous to forgive us our sins and to cleanse us from all unrighteousness" (1 John 1:9). Note that God will remove our sins, forget them (the only One capable of doing so), cause them to vanquish, and erase them. Confession and repentance open the door for His forgiveness.

In the second part of the Model Prayer's fifth petition, Jesus did what He consistently did in His teachings: He stressed that relationship with God is bound up inseparably with our relationships with one another. A person who is not willing to restore a broken relationship with others cannot rightly expect to experience God's forgiveness. It is not that He is unwilling to forgive. The unforgiving have closed the door on God's pardon. One of my New Testament professors in seminary explained it this way: When you close the door on forgiving others, it is closed from both sides; nothing goes out, and nothing comes in. If you do not forgive, you are in no condition to receive forgiveness. As one of my teachers put it, in essence: "The unforgiving are unforgiven because they are unforgivable." The alarmingly tragic truth is that we can render ourselves incapable of receiving God's forgiveness. What we experience from God—His sending away our great debt to Him—we are called on to give to others who have hurt us. Being forgiven and forgiving go together. God's children are to work seriously and consistently at forgiving others.

An offense or debt often is an overt act against someone else. Many injuries we inflict on one another are deliberate acts. Some are motivated by a desire to manipulate others for our own purposes—to view them as objects instead of persons of worth. Some offences are acts of retaliation for real or perceived slights; others are attempts to demean people to make ourselves look good. When we cheat others, lie about them, or disregard them as beneath us, we not only sin against them, but we also sin against the God who made them in His image.

An offense or debt can take the form of a deliberate act. It can, however, be a sizeable debt we incur by a failure to act. Often, we measure our indebtedness to

God and others in terms of what we have done to or against them. Although we may be reluctant to measure indebtedness in terms of what we have failed to do for others, the Scriptures demand that we do so. James wrote: "It is sin to know the good and yet not do it" (James 4:17). Nowhere did Jesus emphasize this more clearly than He did in Matthew 25. In a remarkable scene of judgment, He condemned the failure to act positively on people's behalf. He pointed to acts that anyone can perform: giving food to the hungry, water to the thirsty, hospitality to strangers, clothing to the ill-clad, and care to the sick and incarcerated. People rightly related to Jesus perform these acts out of relationship with Him. This is one of many Scripture passages that makes me uncomfortable. How much of what Jesus pointed out do I do? How often do I perform acts of kindness, speak words of encouragement, and listen as others verbalize their hurts? I live with the awareness that my debt to God and others is composed of what I have done and what I have left undone. God can and will forgive me, but I must never take His pardon lightly or for granted.

The Model Prayer's fifth petition reminds us that we cannot request what we are unwilling to give. Pardon can be received only by people who are prepared to give it. In Matthew 18:21-35, Jesus related the parable of two debtors. Peter had asked Jesus how many times he was required to forgive someone who sinned against him. Instead of setting a limit, Jesus told the story of a man who owed his king a huge debt the person could not pay. The king ordered that the entire family be sold to pay the debt. The man entreated the king to give him time to pay the debt. In response, the king had compassion and canceled the debt. Freed of his debt, the man collared an individual who owed him a relatively small amount and demanded payment. The debtor begged his creditor for time to pay. The creditor refused and had the debtor imprisoned. When the king learned what had happened, he called the forgiven debtor before him and "handed him over to the jailers to be tortured until he could pay everything that was owed" (Matthew 18:34). Jesus applied the story's lesson clearly and chillingly: "So also my heavenly Father will do to you unless every one of you forgives his brother or sister from your heart" (Matthew 18:35). Jesus used strong words of over-emphasis to highlight the high price of the failure to forgive. Our forgiving one another is no small, light matter to God. To be unforgiving is to incur His judgment.

The unforgiving spirit that harbors grudges, nurtures resentment and hate, and holds on to bitterness is the kind of attitude that walls off God's forgiveness. A solid truth with which we must deal is that if we will not apply God's principle of grace, we are in no condition to receive grace.

Centuries ago, Gregory of Nyssa made a bold, daring declaration: Jesus wants your disposition to be a good example to God! We invite God to imitate us— 'do thou the same as I have done.'"[25] In the Scriptures, we are called on repeatedly to reproduce His spirit or attitude; in the fifth request, we ask Him to respond in our spirit. One of the most important words in the fifth petition is the two-letter Greek term translated "as." It means "in the same manner as."[26] We might paraphrase Jesus' statement: "just like we have already forgiven our debtors." Note that the one praying has already erased debts owed him/her. The words' gravity dictates that we approach them cautiously and repeat them honestly.

On one occasion, General Oglethorpe said to John Wesley, "I never forgive." Wesley replied, "Then I hope, sir, that you never sin."[27] The words, "I will never forgive [him or her] for what [he or she] has done to me" are dangerous words. They keep the door closed on God's forgiveness.

The heavenly Father's forgiveness provides the needed basis for genuine forgiving. When we experience the freedom that comes from being released from

---

[25] Barclay, *The Beatitudes & The Lord's Prayer for Everyman*, p. 238.
[26] Thayer, p. 680.
[27] George Arthur Buttrick, "The Gospel According to Matthew" in *The Interpreter's Bible*, vol. 7, p. 314.

indebtedness to God beyond our ability to pay—when we experience the restoration of a broken relationship with the Source and Sustainer of life—and genuinely understand the sheer grace being extended, we are disposed to forgive others.

Note carefully the phrase "as we have also forgiven." Before approaching God for grace, people who understand and appreciate that grace extend grace to people in debt to them. Luke wrote: "for we ourselves also forgive everyone in debt to us." The term "everyone" heightens the demand that believers be forgiving. In the background is the truth that some wrongs are easier to forgive than others. Yet we cannot exercise selective forgiveness.

We must be clear on an important point: Our forgiving others is not the ground of our being forgiven. That is, we cannot say to God: "I have forgiven others; thus, you are bound to forgive me." Rather, the person whose attitude is such that that he/she can dismiss inflicted injuries is conditioned to receive God's forgiveness. The person who refuses to forgive creates a barrier that prevents the receipt of pardon.

"Forgive us our debts, as we also have forgiven our debtors," Jesus taught His disciples to pray. We must constantly be aware that involved in Christian growth is the struggle to be forgiving and the openness to receive forgiveness. Being forgiven and forgiving are two sides of the same coin. Neither can be neglected. We sin and need God to dismiss that debt. Others hurt us, and we need to dismiss their debts. That is one of the creative tensions in which we live as God's children.

A Sobering Elaboration

"For if you forgive others their offences, your heavenly Father will forgive you as well. But if you don't forgive others, your Father will not forgive your offences" (Matthew 6:14-15).

As noted earlier, Jesus expanded on only one petition in the Model Prayer: the request for forgiveness and the accompanying necessity to be forgiving. Although verses 14-15 are not a part of the prayer-pattern Jesus gave, His elaboration stresses the crucial nature of the matter of forgiveness. Jesus used the same word for forgiveness that He used in verse 12, a term that has the idea of letting go, of sending away. The term translated "offences," however, is different from the one earlier translated as "debts." The word in verses 14-15 means "falling to one side, a lapse or deviation from truth or uprightness."[28] It has the sense of "reckless and willful sin....It does not, therefore, imply...excuse. It is a conscious violation of right, involving guilt."[29] Jesus had in mind willful, malicious wrongs against a person.

The form of the phrase "if you forgive others" expresses a condition that is undetermined but has the prospect of being fulfilled. That is, forgiving conscious,

---

[28] Robertson, p. 55.
[29] Marvin R. Vincent, "The Gospel According to Matthew" in *Word Studies in the New Testament*, vol. 1. p. 44.

deliberate wrongs against us is a possibility, but the decision to do so is up to us. Making the conscious decision to let go of those hurtful acts makes possible God's letting go of our deliberate wrongs. As indicated in the treatment of the Model Prayer's fifth petition, the phrases "will forgive" and "will not forgive" do not refer to God's willingness or unwillingness to remove our willful wrongs; they refer to His not being able to forgive us because we have shut the door on forgiveness. If we will not open the door of our lives to allow forgiveness to flow to people who have wronged us, forgiveness cannot enter. God's forgiveness cannot penetrate the barrier built by our stubborn refusal to forgive. To experience forgiveness, we must forgive. We must be open to receive and to give. God is willing and ready to forgive; we must we ready to receive forgiveness by being open to forgive others.

In an earlier book *(The Beatitudes: A Profile of the King's Subject)*, I acknowledged that for me, forgiveness is a process. It begins with my not wanting to get even (or more) with people who have hurt me. It continues as I work through the pain and anger to the point that the memories of the incidents no longer are charged with emotion. The process is complete when I can let go of the incident and the resentment it fostered. As God's child, I live under His demand that I diligently work out the process of forgiving.

An illustration from life is helpful to me as I work at forgiving others. At various times, I have accidentally cut myself. At first, the blood flows freely from the wound. With the proper attention, it begins to heal over. Finally, with continued attention, only a scar is left. Looking at the scar may remind me of the event, but the sight of it no longer ignites pain or disgust with myself. In much the same way, I come to the point of letting go of the injuries others have inflicted on me. The scars may remain, but the wound has healed.

As I stated in the earlier book, I do not believe the adage that we have not forgiven wrongs against us until we have forgotten them is correct. Memory is tricky; some things are imbedded so deeply that from time-to-time, words or scenes or events will call to mind past injuries. I do not believe we can will ourselves to forget. I am convinced that when we remember past wrongs against us without anger or bitterness, we have let the wrongs go.

When we forgive, we experience a freedom that allows us to get on with our lives. The person with an unforgiving spirit remains a prisoner by choice.

Pleading for Protection

"And do not bring us into temptation but deliver us from the evil one" (Matthew 6:13).

On the surface, the sixth and final petition in the Model Prayer is the most puzzling. After the acknowledgment that God is Father in the ultimate sense and is supremely elevated above us, the first three petitions have to do with reverence for Him, submission to His sovereignty, and participation in His redemptive purpose. The Model then turns to the believers' praying for their needs: their need for provision and for forgiveness and being forgiven. The last petition is a plea for protection from temptation and evil.

Jesus taught His disciples to pray, "And do not bring us into temptation." The word "and" links together closely people's primary, crucial needs: the need for bread (daily provision), for being pardoned and pardoning, and for protection from destructive forces. The Greek term translated "bring" has the sense of placing someone or something into some situation. It can have the sense of leading someone into a situation. The idea is "do not cause us to enter" into temptation. The Greek term translated "temptation" means "test" or "trial" in the sense of putting to the proof as well as a pull to evil.[30]

No matter how we interpret the petition, "do not bring us into temptation," one truth is clear: God does not tempt His children (or anyone else) to commit sin. I do not believe He will place any person in the magnetic pull to commit wrong in order to determine how that individual will respond.

I firmly believe that the Father never faces His children with the possibility of giving in to evil in order to develop in them moral muscle. Whenever and wherever such possibilities arise, they are not from God. They can and do arise in the course of following Christ faithfully. James 1:13-15 states: "No one undergoing a trial should say, 'I am being tempted by God,' since God is not tempted by evil, and he himself doesn't tempt anyone. But each person is tempted when he is drawn away and enticed by his own evil desire. Then after desire has conceived, it gives birth to sin, and when sin is full grown, it gives birth to death." That is a rather clear, emphatic statement. When temptation comes, we cannot say it is one way God tests us. Granted, temptation is a test, but it is not God who places the temptation before us.

---

[30] Thayer, p. 498.

Far from tempting us, God is present to help us when we are tempted. Paul wrote: "No temptation has come upon you except what is common to humanity. But God is faithful; he will not allow you to be tempted beyond what you are able, but with the temptation he will also provide a way out so that you may be able to bear it" (1 Corinthians 10:13).

I am convinced that we must take responsibility for allowing temptation to develop into the commission of evil. To me, temptation is being presented with alternatives, good and bad. Temptations are not themselves sin; choosing the wrong alternative is to sin. When we choose wrongly, I do not believe we can blame other people, circumstances, poor upbringing, our environment, or society as a whole. We cannot shift blame from ourselves. Years ago, a popular television comedian popularized the exclamation "the devil made me do it" to excuse a bad action. We cannot use his excuse; we have freedom of choice and can choose to resist temptation. We are responsible for the extent to which anyone or anything influences us; we always reach a point of decision when we give a "yes" or a "no" to a pull to wrong.

Alcoholism well may be a sickness when the individual becomes a victim with no control over the drive to drink, but at some point, the person made a moral choice and said "yes" to the pull to drink alcoholic beverages. The drug addict may no longer have the power to control the use of drugs, but at some point, the person chose to experiment and started down the path to addiction. The same is true for any addiction; they all began with a wrong moral choice. To come down hard on addiction, however, may be easy for those of us who are not addicts. How about selfishness, self-absorption, and self-centeredness, which begin with a conscious decision to put ourselves and our interests above all else? How about greed, which begins with a choice to get ours and more, even at others' expense? How about a drive for prominence and power over others, which starts with a decision to ascend the ladder of success by making compromises with principles and by stepping on and over others on our way up? In these cases, we could choose self-giving, generosity, and service to others—the right alternatives.

The Greek word translated "temptation" can also mean "trial" or "test." With that translation, the request would be that God not put the person praying to the test, that He not "try our faith." As you no doubt know from your experience as a Christian, our faith is tested repeatedly as we make our way through life's minefield. That I come to a clear understanding of how I am tested is crucial. I long have been convinced God never places us in a situation in which we or others may fail the test and be hurt. Jesus once used the method of moving from the lesser to the greater to make His point. "Who among you, if his son asks him for bread, will give him a stone? Or if he asks for a fish, will give him a snake? If you then, who are evil, know how to give good gifts to your children, how much more will your Father in heaven give good things to those who ask him?" (Matthew 7:9-11). Good fathers do everything they can to protect their children from harm. As a father, I never entertained the thought of placing my children in situations of real danger—situations that presented the real possibility they would be hurt—to determine how smart, strong, or courageous they were. If a situation carried even the slightest chance of injury to them, I never put them there. If I, with all my flaws, was so protective of them, how much more does God care for us and how much more does He will only good for us? God is much wiser and much more loving than any earthly father. What I would never do to my children, I cannot believe God would do to us. Life has its multiple threats and dangers, but I don't believe they come from God.

I firmly believe, however, that God does test us. Yet I believe His tests of our faith, love, and faithfulness are always challenges to positive good. People cross our paths, people to whom we can relate in kindness and to whom we can minister in genuine care. They are tests of our love for God and for people. God leads us to situations that need a healing influence we can exert.

These test the depth of our concern. He gives us insight concerning what we should be attempting for Him through His church. Such insight tests our faithfulness. Always, I am convinced, He puts us to the test by our encounters with possibilities of positive good we can do.

I have been helped in understanding the first part of the final petition by a suggestion I came across during my academic journey. In the time of Jesus, some religiously self-confident people were unwise in their conceit and in essence asked of God: "Try me, so I may prove to you what a morally, spiritually strong person I am." Jesus well may have been saying to His disciples—and saying to us today: "Don't pray that prayer." His words remain a strong warning against spiritual arrogance, the false feeling that we are invulnerable, the sense that we have arrived spiritually.

We need to take seriously the truth that in a real sense we will be in a state of siege all our lives. We will never be able to avoid treacherous places in life. We will need to make Jesus' words our own repeatedly as we experience strong pulls to wrong. Repeatedly, New Testament writers referred to life's hard places—to tight corners and threatening pressures. They also expressed strong confidence in God's available grace to sustain.

I find a tremendous source of encouragement in what we are given of Jesus' life and ministry. The writer of Hebrews declared that Jesus was "tempted in every way as we are, yet without sin" (Hebrews 4:15). He entered fully our struggle against temptation and evil, gave Himself no advantage, and yet won the struggle, which was every bit as real as ours. In fact, His temptations were infinitely stronger than any we have faced or will face. His public ministry was one long series of confrontations and crises, yet He consistently called on an inner strength which, as I understand the New Testament, is also available to us.

The final plea in the Model Prayer is for deliverance from "the evil one." Luke did not include this petition in his account. The Greek term behind "deliver" means "to drag out of danger," "to rescue."[31] The final word in the Greek text can be translated "evil" or "the evil one." Interpreters who prefer the latter rendering view the reference to be to the devil or Satan. He is presented as a powerful spirit, a person of evil as God is a Person of good but under God' authority. This evil person approaches people in order to entice them to commit sin and to remain apart from God.

A second view is that the last word in the Model Prayer's final petition is "evil" and conveys the idea of

---

[31] *The Analytical Greek Lexicon*, p. 360.

an impersonal force so malignant and destructive that it is personified. Whatever view we take, I think any rational, observant, sensitive person must admit that evil is an absolute, pervasive, devastating reality. Even a swift, casual survey of history—history as recent as this morning—shows us that a malignant force is present and active in our world. So much exists that is horrifyingly counter to the highest quality of living we know and does violence to any sane standard of behavior. War and its atrocities, crimes of violence, hatred, prejudice, "loophole living"—these realities and more point to a truth beyond debate: Evil is a devastating presence that cannot be explained away.

George A. Buttrick wrote: "The wrong in the world is not merely economic or psychological maladjustment, though these factors may be present: it is wickedness."[32] We dare not close our eyes to the reality of devastating, malignant wrong that cripples and destroys; and we cannot dismiss it as religious myth. We do so at our own peril. Rather, as Jesus emphatically pointed out, we must ask for divine protection from evil. Protection, help, and rescue are available to us, or else Jesus never would have instructed His followers to ask for them. To pray, "Do not bring us into temptation, but deliver us from the evil one (or the evil) is to commit our way to the Father

---

[32] Buttrick, p. 315.

who loves us and makes available grace and strength in the face of pulls to evil.

I have wondered whether Jesus may have had in mind another use of the word "evil." A Hebrew term that appears frequently in the Old Testament means "evil, distress, misery, injury, calamity."[33] In the Genesis account of Joseph's response to his brothers' having sold him into slavery in Egypt, he used the word to express the injury and distress they had inflicted on him: "You planned evil against me; but God planned it for good to bring about the present result—the survival of many people" (Genesis 50:20). If this idea lay underneath Jesus' meaning in His prayer outline, He could have instructed His followers to pray that God would not put them to the test but to protect them from harm or distress. If so, we can legitimately pray for divine protection for ourselves and others.

William Barclay wrote: "This concluding petition of the Lord's Prayer does three things. First, it frankly faces the danger of the human situation. Second, it freely confesses the inadequacy of human resources to deal with it. Thirdly, its takes both the danger and the weakness to the protecting power of God."[34] When we

---

[33] Francis Brown, S. R. Driver, and Charles Briggs, *A Hebrew and English Lexicon of the Old Testament,* p. 948.
[34] Barclay, *The Beatitudes & The Lord's Prayer for Everyman,* p. 253.

humbly, sincerely include this petition in our prayers, we open our lives to receive God's enabling power.

Offering a Concluding Doxology

"For thine is the kingdom, and the power, and the glory, forever. Amen" (Matthew 6:13b; KJV).[35]

By separate notes or the use of brackets, various translations of Matthew indicate that the doxology included in the King James Version was a later addition to the Model Prayer. Frank Stagg wrote: "The beautiful and cherished doxology…is by all indications not original to Matthew. It is not in Luke. It appears as early as the Didache (early second century) in a short form, 'For thine is the power and the glory forever.' It also appeared in various manuscripts in other short forms and finally emerged in the long form widely known today, modeled apparently on 1 Chronicles 29:11f."[36] The writer of 1 Chronicles declared: "Yours, Lord, is the greatness and the power and the glory and the splendor and the majesty, for everything in the heavens and on earth belongs to you. Yours, Lord, is the kingdom, and you are exalted as head overall. Riches and honor come from you, and you are the ruler of everything" (1 Chronicles 29:11-12).

One suggestion is that early Christians added the doxology in the course of using the Model Prayer in worship. The continued use of it in repeating the

---

[35] *The Holy Bible: King James Version*, p. 858.
[36] Stagg, "Matthew," p. 116.

prayer has drawn contrasting opinions. John A. Broadus, a Southern Baptist scholar of a past generation, wrote: "We may give up the pleasing and familiar words with regret, but surely it is more important to know what the Bible really contains and really means, than to cling to something not really in the Bible, merely because it gratifies our taste, or even because it has for us some precious associations."[37] Others contend it is a legitimate conclusion, calling it "a thoroughly Christian statement"[38] and "a very appropriate conclusion" that "no one need campaign to do away with its use in churches today."[39] I do not recall a time when the doxology was not included as I joined in a corporate recitation of the Model Prayer.

Whoever wrote the doxology (a statemen of praise)—perhaps a copyist—did an excellent job in the brief but exceedingly beautiful conclusion. The term "for" connects what follows with the previous petitions concerning God and His people. The word "thine" (yours) has the force of "yours and yours alone." Three areas are ascribed to God's supreme, absolute possession. First, God is absolute Ruler; He is sovereign over all that exists and in a special sense over

---

[37] John A. Broadus, "Commentary on the Gospel of Matthew" in *An American Commentary on the New Testament*, p. 139.
[38] Tolbert, p. 59.
[39] Craig L. Blomberg, "Matthew" in *The New American Commentary*, vol. 22, p. 121.

people who have submitted to His rule through faith in Christ. Second, God has absolute power. The Greek word has the sense of ability, authority, and energy. God is more than able to accomplish His purposes. Third, God's glory is inherent and is to be recognized. The Greek term has the ideas of magnificence, splendor, majesty, and radiance. In addition, it has the sense of God's self-revealed character as redemptive.

An unknown writer gave a marvelous expression of praise to God, who wants to become Father to people who desperately need His mercy and grace. He is worthy of our exaltation.

Conclusion: Thoughts on Prayer

How would you chronicle your spiritual journey in the area of prayer? Mine got off to the shakiest possible start. The first time I remember praying was in a group of boys in Training Union. Our teacher called on me to pray, and I was totally unprepared. I attempted to quote a Scripture verse and botched it. Later, my Sunday School teacher, who also was the high school math teacher, helped me learn to pray in a group. Evidently, I made some progress. One day in school assembly, he called on me to pray. That was one of the scariest moments in my young life. Since that time, numerous pastors, seminary teachers, and devotional writers have helped my development in praying. Two housewives put their prayers in everyday (and sometimes humorous) phrasing. John Ballie's book *A Diary of Private Prayer* broadened my horizons in my praying. Listening to laypersons' prayers has enriched mine. At this point, late in life, I am still in process.

To me, prayer is conversation with God—talking *with* God. My problem is that most often, I talk *to* Him; my prayers are monologues rather than dialogues. I fail to wait for His responses. He has never communicated with me in an audible voice, but sometimes a thought forms, or I feel a nudge or an impulse to do something for someone who is hurting. Some of my prayers are answered; some are still pending and may not receive the answer I would like. As you no doubt have, I have heard that God answers prayers in three ways: yes, no, and wait a while. I have been introduced to two additional possibilities: "You've got to be kidding!" and "I thought you'd never ask!" I have learned to acknowledge in my prayers that God will answer according to His infinite wisdom, and that is good enough for me.

Prayer includes asking, as the Model Prayer makes clear. We can express our petitions for God's help. Yet much more is involved. At the top of the list of elements is gratitude. I often itemize items for which I am thankful, but I can never identify and include all the blessings and benefits that come to me as God's child. I am grateful for life—each day that comes as a gift of grace and length of life marked by opportunities of service and populated with people who offered friendship and enriched my life. I am grateful for new life in Christ made possible by God's great gift of salvation at immeasurable cost to Himself. That thought brings with it awe and amazement at God's incomprehensible grace, love, and mercy.

Praise is a part of my praying. The God who drew me into His circle of grace deserves my continuing praise for who He is—the heavenly Father who cares about me, as insignificant as I am. Part of my praying is that my life be a daily expression of praise.

Intercession is a vital and necessary part of prayer. We have the opportunity to pray for others' needs. Dietrich Bonhoeffer wrote: "A Christian fellowship lives and exists by the intercession of its members for one another, or it collapses....Intercession means no more than to bring our brother into the presence of God, to see him under the Cross of Jesus as a poor human being and sinner in need of grace."[40] As members of the community of faith, we have the high privilege and daily responsibility of placing one another by name in the center of God's grace.

I view my praying as celebration. I celebrate the aspects of God's character as I understand them: love, grace, mercy, patience, kindness, compassion, generosity, and faithfulness. From the pages of the Scriptures, and more specifically from Jesus' life and ministry, I celebrate what I know about God and His stance toward me as His child—undeserving but needy and loved.

To me, prayer is a form of worship. When I pray, I view myself as deliberately entering God's presence as humbly and reverently as I can. I acknowledge I can so only because He invites me to approach Him. Prayer is a gift of His grace by which I can address Him

---

[40] Dietrich Bonhoeffer, *Life Together*, p. 86.

anywhere, at any time, in the confidence He hears me out of His care for me.

I have a lot to learn about prayer. My aim is to stay open to learn. The Model Prayer will remain my guide. I will continue to work to make it mine, so it is authentic, sincere prayer repeated with meaning.

Postscript

The incident may have been mere coincidence, but I wonder. I had finished the second draft of my manuscript and had printed it. I placed the pages on my desk to let them "cool" for a spell before I did a final reading to correct, add to, subtract from, and polish the finished product. Soon after, on a Sunday morning, I entered my church's sanctuary for the worship time. I was late, and someone was singing an arrangement of the Lord's Prayer that was new to me. The soloist had a marvelous voice and did a magnificent job. At the conclusion of his presentation, the congregation applauded. I may have been the only attendee who did not do so. I am confident the people who clapped were sincere in wanting to express their appreciation for the talented singer's work. Yet I wondered how many of us had taken the words to heart and had resolved to redouble our efforts to live out the prayer. How many had become enthralled with the singer's superb voice and had merely mentally recited familiar words?

Two days later, in an entirely different venue, a crowd was asked to join in reciting the prayer Jesus gave. My wife, grandson, and I attended a country music concert benefiting an organization whose mission is to feed hungry people, especially children, in our state. The person leading the prayer had offered her petitions and thanks and then invited audience participation by repeating the Lord's (Model) Prayer. Many (some holding their cups of beer) dutifully repeated the words. And I wondered how many did so perfunctorily. What followed included loud music, sometimes unnecessary swear words, and shady innuendoes. I mentally questioned the appropriateness of placing Jesus' marvelous guide to prayer in such a context.

Jesus' Model Prayer was never meant to be a prelude to or expression of entertainment, whether it be in a religious or a secular context. As I understand it, at least part of Jesus' intention was to give us a reminder of the privilege of relationship with God, of His exalted nature, and of the primacy of His redemptive purpose. Jesus may also have meant to keep before us the reminder that we are needy creatures who can rely on our Father to meet our deepest needs. The prayer demands that we not only know the words but also live by them.

The following is one attempt to use Jesus' guide for our praying:

Our Father, thanks is a woefully feeble word to express our response to your grace that allows us to relate to you and to approach you in prayer, yet along with gratitude it is the best verbal vehicle we have. Thank you for loving us, although we are not lovable, and for accepting us, although we are unacceptable. We humbly acknowledge that we are mere creatures; you are the Creator. We reverence and honor you as Sovereign over your universe and over those of us who have entered your family through faith in Christ.

We take our places in the work of extending your beneficent rule over peoples' lives as they accept your gracious offer of salvation through Christ. We also strive to know and to do your will and to have your will implemented in others' lives.

We acknowledge our dependence on you for existence. We pray that you will meet our needs as we labor to the best of our abilities in the opportunities you give us. Move us to be more generous in helping meet others' needs. We ask that you erase our indebtedness to You as we cancel others' debts to us. We humbly ask that You not test us but that you protect us from evil.

Thank you for being our compassionate Father. Amen.

Selected Bibliography

Allen, Charles L., *God's Psychiatry* (Westwood, N. J: Pyramid Publications, Inc. for the Fleming H. Revell Company, 1953)

Barclay, William, *The Beatitudes and the Lord's Prayer for Everyman* (New York, N. Y.: Harper and Row, Publishers, 1964)

_____, "The Gospel of Matthew," vol. 1, in *The Daily Study Bible* (Philadelphia: The Westminster Press, nd)

Blomberg, Craig L., "Matthew" in *The New American Commentary*, vol. 22 (Nashville, Tennessee: Broadman Press, 1992)

Bonhoeffer, Dietrich, *Life Together* (New York: Harper & Row, Publishers, 1954)

Broadus, John A., "Commentary on the Gospel of Matthew" in *An American Commentary on the New Testament* (Valley Forge, Pa.: The American Baptist Publication Society, 1886)

Brown, Francis, S. R. Driver, and Charles A. Briggs, *A Hebrew and English Lexicon of the Old Testament* (Oxford: Clarendon Press, nd)

Buttrick, George A., "The Gospel According to St. Matthew" in *The Interpreter's Bible*, vol. 7 (Nashville, Tennessee: The Parthenon Press, 1951)

Hunter, Archibald M., *Teaching and Preaching the New Testament* (Philadelphia: The Westminster Press, nd)

Stagg, Frank, "Matthew" in *The Broadman Bible Commentary*, vol. 8 (Nashville: Broadman Press,1969)

_____, *New Testament Theology* (Nashville, Tennessee: Broadman Press, 1962)

Robertson, Archibald Thomas, "The Gospel According to Matthew" in *Word Pictures in the New Testament*, vol. 1 (Nashville, Tennessee: Broadman Press, 1930)

Thayer, Joseph Henry, *A Greek-English Lexicon of the New Testament* (Grand Rapids, Michigan: Zondervan Publishing House, 1970)

The Analytical Greek Lexicon (New York: Harper & Row Publishers, nd)

The Holy Bible: King James Version (Grand Rapids, Michigan: Zondervan Bible Publishers, 1984)

Thielicke, Helmut, *Our Heavenly Father: Sermons on the Lord's Prayer* (New York: Harper & Row, Publishers, 1960)

Tolbert, Malcolm O., *Good News from Matthew,* vol. 1 (Nashville, Tennessee: Broadman Press, 1975)

Vincent, Marvin R., "The Gospel According to Matthew," vol. 1 in *Word Studies in the New Testament* (Grand Rapids, Michigan: Wm. B. Eerdmans Publishing Co., 1965)

Webster's New World Dictionary of the American Language (Nashville, Tenn.: The Southwestern Company, 1969)

www.ingramcontent.com/pod-product-compliance
Lightning Source LLC
Chambersburg PA
CBHW052158110526
44591CB00012B/1995